Comparative Studies
in
History of Religions

# Comparative Studies in History of Religions

Their Aim, Scope, and Validity

Edited by
*Erik Reenberg Sand*
&
*Jørgen Podemann Sørensen*

MUSEUM TUSCULANUM PRESS
UNIVERSITY OF COPENHAGEN
1999

*Comparative Studies in History of Religions*
© Museum Tusculanum Press and the authors, 1999
Cover Design by Henrik Maribo Pedersen
Set in Baskerville
Printed in Denmark by Special-Trykkeriet Viborg a-s
ISBN 87 7289 533 0

The publication of this volume was made possible through a grant from The Danish Research Council for the Humanities *(Statens Humanistiske Forskningsråd).*

For valuable support in the process of editing the volume, the editors want to thank also the University of Copenhagen, Department of History of Religions, and, not least, our friend and colleague Bruce Lincoln, who was very helpful in editing some of the papers.

Museum Tusculanum Press
University of Copenhagen
Njalsgade 92
DK-2300 Copenhagen S.
Denmark
www.mtp.dk

# Contents

Introduction  7

*Lourens P. van den Bosch*
Friedrich Max Müller: His Contribution to the Science of
Religion  *11*

*Bruce Lincoln*
The History of Religions and the History of Authority  *41*

*Britt-Mari Näsström*
Freyja: The Trivalent Goddess  *57*

*Tord Olsson*
Verbal Representation of Religious Beliefs: A Dilemma in the
Phenomenology of Religions  *75*

*William E. Paden*
Reconceiving the Category of the Sacred  *93*

*Erik Reenberg Sand*
Comparative Religion: Between Phenomenology and Typology
of Religions  *109*

*Jens Peter Schjødt*
Typological and Genetic Comparisons: Implications and
Perspectives  *121*

*Jørgen Podemann Sørensen*
Levels of Comparison: A Critical Approach to Thematization in
Comparative Religion  *131*

*Alan V. Williams*
Speaking of Purity: When the Zoroastrian High Priest first met
the Hindu Rajah  *143*

# Introduction

This dossier of papers presented at a conference on the occasion of the 10th anniversary of the Danish Association for the History of Religions in 1992 addresses the fundamental issue of the role of comparative studies in history of religions. Since its beginnings in the second half of the nineteenth century, this discipline has always somehow invoked comparative insights as its very *raison d'être*. The nature of these insights has been under constant debate, within the discipline as well as with scholars from adjacent disciplines. At times, scepticism and devastating critique of the more pretentious comparative projects have discouraged scholars from undertaking comparative enterprises, but the fact remains that the major, general issues addressed by historians of religions are rooted in considerations of a comparative nature.

In his *Introduction to the Science of Religion* (1873), Friedrich Max Müller defined religion as "a mental faculty which, independent of, nay, in spite of sense and reason, enables man to apprehend the infinite under different names and under varying disguises." Notwithstanding its anticipation of more recent cognitive approaches to religion, this definition laid the foundation of comparative studies in religion. For if religion is a human potential common to the whole species, but producing different mythologies, concepts etc. in different areas of the globe, then a true science of religion must devote itself to cross-cultural comparative studies in order to isolate and understand that human potential. This was not, however, the only leading perspective in Max Müller's work. In his paper, L. van den Bosch brings out how much Max Müller's comparative studies were rooted in a historical vision. To him as to later scholars who worked within an evolutionist paradigm, the nature of religion was largely a matter of its origin and growth, and a major objective of his comparative studies was to establish links between the childhood and the maturity of mankind. Although his project was, from the outset, a more universal undertaking, Max Müller focused his studies on the religions of the Aryan nations. Thus, at an early stage, comparative studies in religion assumed certain ideas of historical development and genetic bonds.

Still today, the investigation of genetic bonds between religions and mythologies retains some currency. The Indo-European mythological patterns found by G. Dumézil not only demonstrate historical continuities; as Britt-Mari Näsström shows in her paper, they also have heuristic value in the study of a single Indo-European mythology.

The attempt to understand the religious potential in man and the search for genetic bonds are more intricately intertwined in the evolutionist synthesis of J. G. Frazer who is, more than any other single person, responsible both for the popularity and for the bad reputation of comparative studies in religion. In his well-known theory of homeopathic and contagious magic, Frazer established universal principles related to the human religious potential or faculty. But he took these as mistakes, committed at an early stage of man's development and perpetuated by religious traditions – or, in a more polemic mood, as the "truly catholic creed" of early man. The project of identifying universal patterns was thus subordinated to that of establishing genetic bonds between primitive magic and the religion of his own day.

If Müller and Frazer confused what Jens Peter Schjødt in his paper calls genetic and typological comparisons, the two approaches are found unmixed in Panbabylonism and Phenomenology of Religion respectively. In the light of the diffusionist hypothesis of Panbabylonism, all similarities revealed by comparison were constituted as evidence of the world-wide influence of ancient Babylonian religion. When Panbabylonism was at its height, it seemed only a matter of sufficient ink and paper before the last *Kulturprovinz* would surrender. The Phenomenology of Religion, on the other hand, took the radical position that no cause or common origin could account for the similarities found, except, perhaps, religion itself. Although the classical phenomenologists of religion were thus in a position to reject almost any theory of religion as reductionist, they faced the formidable difficulty of making observations from no situated point of view.

There are at least two ways of escaping this difficulty: One is to consider the phenomenology of religion as a matter of describing and classifying the data. This is the view advocated by Jens Peter Schjødt in his paper. Alternatively, one can choose a key notion or category within religion and study the data as modalities of this principal notion. As is well known, this was the strategy of M. Eliade's "morphology of the sacred". In his paper, William Paden advocates the more modest notion of sacrality as a key category in comparative studies – not as an irreducible *a priori* category, but as a thematic construct with a heuristic value.

Even so, any comparative study restricted neither by a theoretical framework, nor by the historical and socio-cultural contexts of the items compared, will always be open to uncritical compilation around favourite ideas. To remedy the almost programmatic subjectivity of the classical phenomenology of religion, Erik Reenberg Sand suggests that a socio-cultural typology of religions is a necessary framework for the comparative study of single religious phenomena. Since religions are systems that interact with society and culture, he argues, comparatists are obliged to take notice of the systemic and contextual properties of the items compared. Another way to restrict the influence of favourite ideas and arbitrariness in comparative thematic studies, is to distinguish types of religious discourse. The consecration of the host is not a statement of the *belief* that the blessed body of Christ is a biscuit; it is part of a ritual discourse. In his comparative study of Maasai, Egyptian, and Greek verbal representations of gods, Tord Olsson demonstrates the necessity of distinguishing literary genres and speech situations before generalizing about a "conception" of god. What looks like elements of a conception of god to the uncritical compiler of examples may in fact be properties of a literary genre. In similar fashion, J. Podemann Sørensen tries to differentiate types of religious discourse that could direct and restrict comparative studies much as the distinct levels of phonetics, syntax and semantics do in linguistics.

Introduction

In the history of religions, comparative studies are not limited to religious infrastructure, but may, as Bruce Lincoln argues, throw light on broader themes. His own study of authority in the Iliad and in present day political discourse serves to illustrate how comparative studies may remedy tendencies to cut the religious past off radically from secular modernity. Like authority, the recurring theme of ethnic identity in Alan Williams' paper on Zoroastrian purity rules is one that occurs also in secular settings and certainly an important issue in the study of contemporary history. Neither the past nor the present is unique.

Perhaps this applies to the history of our comparative discipline as well. The testimony, not the conclusion, of the present volume is that comparative studies – now more varied, more critical about their own scope and validity, and less bound to monolithic visions of history and human nature – are still of fundamental importance in history of religions. It was Max Müller who coined the famous motto of the comparative study of religion: "He who knows one, knows none" – now rephrased by Bruce Lincoln in terms of a general epistemological condition: "Fish, I would argue, do not begin to know water until they break the surface of their liquid environs and for the first time encounter air ..."

Erik Reenberg Sand					Jørgen Podemann Sørensen

# Friedrich Max Müller: His Contribution to the Science of Religion

*Lourens P. van den Bosch*
UNIVERSITY OF GRONINGEN, THE NETHERLANDS

Friedrich Max Müller (1823-1900) was a scholar of international reputation who left a distinct mark on discourse in the humanities during the second half of the nineteenth century.[1] His books and lectures, which were frequently reprinted and translated into many languages, held theories on the origin and development of language, mythology, religion, and thought that not only drew the attention of scholars, but also struck the imagination of a wider public. His search for origins was consistent with the new ideas of his time which centered on evolution and history. Without affecting essential notions of Christianity, he offered idealistic alternatives to the educated public which were in tune with the modern sensibilities. At his death many sovereigns, princes, political and cultural dignitaries sent their condolences to his wife.[2] Also many modern Indians mourned for the death of the man who had contributed so much to the study of ancient Indian culture and had returned to India some of its age-old texts. His edition of the *Rigveda* with the voluminous commentary of Sāyana (Müller 1849-1874) is still regarded as a model for a scien-

---
1. The autobiographical data are mentioned in Müller 1901a and G. Müller 1902. A biography based on the Müller Archives in the Bodleian Library (Oxford), is Chaudhuri 1974. For other short descriptions see e.g. Sharpe 1975: 35-46; Trompf 1978; Neufeldt 1980: 2-18.
2. For a survey see the Bodleian Library Archives, MS. Eng. d. 2365-6. Cf. also Chaudhuri 1974: 2-4.

tific edition of a religious text. Andrew Lang, his main critic in the field of mythology and religion, praised him in his obituary for the humor and friendliness with which he met his opponents.[3] The fame Müller received during his lifetime sharply contrasts with his posthumous decline. Among scholars in comparative religion he is best remembered as the principal editor of the series *Sacred Books of The East*.[4] Nonetheless, his contributions to the science of religion were of such fundamental importance for the establishment of this branch of study as an academic discipline that he is nowadays regarded as its founder.[5]

## 1. Life and Works

The contributions of Max Müller to the science of religion were strongly moulded by the cultural and philosophic milieu of the German schools and universities where he received his education. Müller was trained in the humanities, especially in Greek and Latin, at the famous Nicolai school in Leipzig, which counted Leibniz as one of its most renowned pupils. At the Leipzig university Müller studied German literature, Sanskrit, Arabic, history, and philosophy.[6] After his dissertation on the third book of Spinoza's Ethics in 1843, he went to Berlin where he attended lectures by F. von Schelling on the philosophy of mythology, by F. Bopp on the comparative grammar of the Indo-European languages, and by F. Rückert on the Persian language. Schelling aroused Müller's interests in the evolution of religious and philosophical thought and stimulated him to study the an-

---

3. Lang 1900: 784-93; see also G. Müller 1902, II: 452-3.
4. Müller expounded the principal aims of the *Sacred Books of the East* in the preface of the first volume of 1879. Until 1904 a total of 51 volumes were published.
5. For a discussion of his position as 'father of comparative religion', see e.g. Jordan 1905: 521-3; Rudolph 1962: 12 ff.; Waardenburg 1973, I: 13 f.; Sharpe 1975: XI-III, 35-46; Kitagawa and Strong 1985: 179-85.
6. Müller 1901a: 120-22; Chaudhuri 1974: 78-82. See also MS. Germ. d. 23 in the Bodleian Library with parts of the notes from the lectures in Leipzig.

cient Sanskrit texts as well as Indian philosophy and religion. In 1845, he went to Paris where, at the Collège de France, Eugène Burnouf initiated him in the study of the *Rigveda* which would become of vital importance for his understanding of religion in its germinal stage.[7] Burnouf advised him to prepare a critical edition of the *Rigveda* with Sāyana's commentary. He left Paris for London through the intercession of Horace H. Wilson, professor of Sanskrit in Oxford and curator of the Oriental manuscripts of the East India Company, to collect the most important manuscripts for this edition. Müller settled in Oxford in 1847 and in 1854, he became professor of modern European languages at the Taylor Institute which was closely associated with the University of Oxford.[8] Nonetheless, the study of ancient Indian texts and culture, especially from a comparative point of view, had his first interest.[9] In 1856 he published the influential *Essay on Comparative Mythology*,[10] in which he tried to find a solution for the many riddles in ancient Greek mythology with the help of the etymological method of Indo-European philology; a method that, subsequently, were to become very controversial.[11]

Müller was greatly disappointed when he was passed over for the vacancy of the Boden Chair of Sanskrit at Oxford in favor of M. Monier Williams. An important reason seems to have been his supposed liberal theological ideas[12] which were especially con-

---

7. Müller 1901a: 172-4. For his meeting with Dwarkanath Tagore in Paris (who brought him in contact with many representatives of Hinduism), see Müller 1898-9, II: 5 ff. See further Chaudhuri 1974, 50-3.
8. See e.g. G. Müller 1902, I: 55 ff.; Chaudhuri 1974: 109-11.
9. See e.g. Müller 1859: 7-9; 1883: 1-27, esp. 6 and 14 ff. Cf. also Chaudhuri 1974: 134 f.; Neufeldt 1980: 11-5.
10. For more recent critical evaluations of Müller's work on mythology, see e.g. Dorson 1965: 25-63 and 1968: 161-175; Stocking 1987: 57-62.
11. See e.g. his lecture delivered in 1870 at the Royal Institution: 'On the Philosophy of Mythology', published in Müller 1873: 335-442, esp. 352-3. Cf. also Neufeldt 1980: 62-91 and paragraph 3 below (mythology).
12. G. Müller I, 1902: 252-4; Chaudhuri 1974: 220-8. See also Encyclopaedia Britannica, ed. 1911, sub: Max Müller. The correspondence on this subject is found in the Bodleian Library (Oxford) MS. Eng. c. 2807.

nected with Germany where the Tübingen school flourished with scholars as F. C. Baur and D.F. Strauss.[13] He subsequently turned his attention to comparative philology and gave two series of lectures at the Royal Institute on the science of language to the social and intellectual élite of London.[14] Here he introduced ideas on Indo-European languages and a comparative historical grammar originally worked out by German scholars such as Bopp, J. Grimm and others. These lectures were published and brought him great fame. In 1868, he was appointed by the university of Oxford to the newly created chair for comparative philology,[15] but his attention had again shifted and he now devoted more attention to the comparative study of religion. This resulted in a series of lectures for the Royal Institute in 1870 which were published in 1873 as *Introduction to the Science of Religion*. In this book, he developed his main ideas on the comparative approach.[16] Müller elaborated his theories on the origin and development of religion in the Hibbert lectures, 1878, in which he used materials derived from the Vedas, and published them under the title: *Lectures on the Origin and Growth of Religion, as Illustrated by the Religions of India*. Here, he also dealt with ethnological problems related to the origin of religion and criticized the concept of fetishism as used by ethnologists in their reconstruction of the origin of religious life.[17]

---

13. For the position of Baur and Strauss see e.g. R. Morgan 1985, I: 265-89; H. Frei 1985, I: 215-60.
14. Müller had held lectures on comparative philology at the Taylorian Institute (Oxford) since 1851 which were quite succesful; see the Bodleian Library, MS. Eng. d. 2353. The publications of the 1861 and 1864 lectures were the fruit of many years of reflection. They were reprinted fourteen times before 1886.
15. Müller 1861 and 1864. For his appointment to the chair, see Chaudhuri 1974: 230. The title of his inaugural lecture of 1868 runs, 'On the value of comparative philology as a branch of academic study', Müller 1867-1875, IV: 1 ff.
16. Müller 1873. The expression 'Comparative Religion' was used by Müller for the first time in 1867; see Müller 1867[1] in the preface to his *Chips of a German Workshop* I. See also Berkenkopf 1914: 2; Sharpe 1975: 32 note 7.
17. Müller 1878: 54 ff. Müller writes in his unpublished diary on 3 october 1878, 'I like it best of all my books, but I know that it will be misunderstood and ill-treated'; Bodleian Library, MS. Eng. d. 2364, paroksha 16.

From the beginning of his study in Leipzig, Müller had always had a keen interest in philosophical matters.[18] Immanuel Kant especially attracted his attention on account of his epistemological ideas which proved to be fruitful for Müller's theories on language where he took a stand against Darwin and his followers.[19] In 1881 he published an English translation of Kant's *Kritik der reinen Vernunft* and formulated his opinion on the relation between the Vedas and Kant as follows:

> The bridge of thoughts and sighs that spans the whole history of the Aryan world has its first arch in the *Vedas*, its last in Kant's *Critique*. While in the Veda we may study childhood, we may study in Kant's *Critique of Pure Reason* the perfect manhood of the Aryan mind.[20]

With these words, he made it clear that he regarded the ancient documents of the Aryans also as documents of the origin of the western civilization and used them in his reconstruction of the development of the Western mind, with Kant as its pinnacle. In

---

18. In the winter semester of 1842-1843 Müller, among others, attended courses in metaphysics and philosophy of history; cf. Bodleian Library, MS. Germ. d. 23. Moreover, he participated in a seminar on Kant given by H. Lotze. Müller relates in his autobiography that Herbart's philosophy, as taught by Drobisch in Leipzig, came as a most useful antidote against the Hegelianism of Weisse; Müller 1901a: 136-7. Herbart's method of analysis and clarification of concepts was applied by Müller to the historical study of language and religion and various religious concepts; see e.g. Müller 1878: 1-54 with an analysis of various definitions of religion and 54-131 with an analysis of the concept of fetishism; Müller 1890: chapters III-V again on the definition of religion and 126-9 on the concept of mana. See also Kitagawa and Strong 1985: 190-1.
19. See Müller 1887: 127 ff. (chapter 3: 'On Kant's Philosophy'); For a short discussion on the relation between Kant and Müller, see Kitagawa and Strong 1985: 192-6.
20. Müller in G. Müller 1902, II: 121-2. See also idem, II: 115 which quotes the preface to his translation of Kant's *Critique* of 1881 and his letter to Malabari, d.d. 29 january 1882. See further Müller 1901b: 218-50 with the extracts of the preface to his translation of 1881.

1882, in a series of lectures at the University of Cambridge subsequently published as *India, what can it teach us?*, he devoted more attention to the present situation of India. He wished to show candidates of the Indian Civil Services the ways in which the Indian character and outlook could be complementary to those of the European. In this context, he especially stressed the importance of the study of Sanskrit for recovery of an ancient chapter of history of the Indo-European people.[21]

In the following years, he elaborated his theories on the relation between language and thought subsequently published as *Science of Thought,* 1887. He placed himself in the tradition of Nominalism but qualified his theories as Nominism, 'because it aims at determining the origin and the true nature of names'.[22]

In his four series of *Gifford Lectures* at the university of Glasgow, 1888-1892, Müller developed a philosophy of religion which claimed to be based on the comparative study of religion. Central in his philosophy was the idea that an independent study of the religions of the world, if properly understood, taught us a lesson, namely the divine education of the human race.[23] In the spirit of Lord Adam Gifford, Müller aimed to trace Natural Religion as presented in the growth of the principal religions of the world.[24] The first series of lectures was devoted to a general introduction to Natural Religion and published under the same title in 1889. It dealt with definitions of religion, clarification of concepts, the value of religious texts and the methods to be used when dealing with such texts. In them Müller wanted to show that his 'preliminary definition of religion in its widest sense, namely the Perception of the Infinite, can be shown by

---

21. See Müller 1883: 1, 5 f. and 15 ff. See also Chaudhuri 1974: 303-4.
22. See Müller 1887: X. See also his short expositions in 1901b: 63-84: 'Can we think without words?' [or. publ. 1989] and 85-109: 'On Thought and Language' [or. publ. 1891]). See further Moncalm 1900. For a short evaluation of his theories, see also Neufeldt 1980: 123-55.
23. Müller 1873: 226. See Bosch 1998.
24. Müller 1893: 89. For the religious ideas of Adam Gifford, see Müller 1889: preface VII- XIV; lecture I.

historical evidence to have been the one element shared in common by all religions'.[25] The discovery of God, of the Soul, and of the oneness of God and the Soul were the principal themes of the three following series of lectures.[26] Müller tried to sketch these themes in the evolution of religious thinking and devoted to each of them a publication, namely *Physical Religion* (1891), *Anthropological Religion* (1892), and lastly *Theosophy or Psychological Religion* (1893). Psychological or Theosophic religion presupposed, according to Müller, both Physical and Anthropological religion because both the concept of God and the soul had to be elaborated before they could be brought in relation to each other. God had to be conceived as soul-like and the soul of man as God-like.[27]

Müller decided to elucidate – and adapt – his former ideas on mythology in his voluminous *Contributions to the Science of Mythology*.[28] His main reasons to do so were the fierce attacks in the preceding decades by ethnologists and folklorists among whom A. Lang is the most well-known.[29] Müller tried again to underpin the validity of the etymological method in the study of mythology, though he acknowledged the value of other methods. His last publications were devoted to personal memories (Müller 1898-9b), to the Indian mystic Ramakrishna, and to the six traditional systems of Indian philosophy (Müller 1898a and 1899a). During the final years of his life Müller was highly honoured by Queen Victoria who appointed him to the Privy Council; but he realized that his ideas in many respects had become outdated. The science of language, the science of mythology, and the science of religion had taken directions other than those he had in mind. After his death in 1900, a Cornish cross was placed on his grave on Holywell Cemetery (Oxford) with his motto through life: 'Wie Gott will'.[30]

---

25. Müller 1893: Preface VII; see also lecture IV, esp 88-91.
26. Müller 1893: Preface I.
27. Müller 1893: 91.
28. Müller 1897, 2 vols.
29. Lang 1884: 135-57, esp. 137-41. See also paragraph 3.
30. G. Müller 1902, II: 451.

## 2. Language

Language occupied a central position in the understanding of Müller's ideas on mythology, religion and philosophy.[31] In this respect, he worked in the tradition of German Romanticism with scholars such as Johan Gottfried von Herder, Friedrich von Schlegel and Wilhelm von Humboldt.[32] For them, language was not only a means of communication but also a constitutive for, and an expressive of, human thought.[33] Language and thought were both sides of the same coin, as it were, and indissolubly connected to each other.[34] Hegel and Schelling had developed these ideas and stressed the close interrelation between language, nation (*ethnos*) and religion.[35] For Müller, the notion that thought expressed itself in language implied that the development of the human mind could be studied in the development of language.[36] The comparative study of the Indo-European languages by scholars such as Bopp and Jacob Grimm were of paramount importance for Müller when he elaborated his ideas.[37] By means of

---

31. For a systematic exposition of his ideas see Müller 1887: esp. 77 ff. (chapter 2: 'Thought and Language') and 152 ff. (chapter 4: 'Language and the Barrier between Man and Beast'). See further idem: 299: 'Language has created Reason, and that before there was language, man was without reason'. For a short evaluation of his linguistic theories see, Jankowski 1979: 346 ff.; Olender 1992: 82-92. For an older survey see Moncalm 1900.
32. Müller 1861, I: 184-86.
33. For a survey of the theories of scholars such as Herder, Renan and Müller see, e.g., Olender 1992: 31-36; especially 37-50 (Herder), 51-81 (Renan), 82-92 (Müller). For Von Humboldt, see De Pater 1986: 210-232. For an older survey, employed by Müller, see Steinthal 1858².
34. For a short description of his position see, Müller 1901b: 1-25; 63-84; 85-109 with three essays on this subject.
35. See e.g. Müller 1887: 45, 145 ff; Müller 1891b, vol. II: 83.
36. See also Herder 1895, V: 52: 'Und was ist also die ganze Bauart der Sprache anders als eine Entwickelungsweise seines Geistes, eine Geschichte seiner Entdeckungen!'
37. Bopp 1816: 1833-52 (eng. ed. 1845-53); Grimm 1819-37; see Müller 1866 [1861], I: 184 f. for theories of Bopp and 1864; and II: 198 ff. for Grimm's law in the field of Indo-European phonetics.

the various Indo-European languages, Müller and his supporters tried to reconstruct the oldest stage and common language *(Ursprache)* of the Aryans *(Urvolk)*. The discovery of the common linguistic heritage led to a break-through in the reconstruction of the past. In this context, Müller spoke about a 'paleontology of the human mind' and was of the opinion that the true history of the human mind could only be read in the records of language.[38] He stated that a classification of religion according to a classification of languages was justified because religion in the earliest phase of mankind was totally dependent on language in its outward expression. Müller reconstructed three early 'oases' (niches) of language, the Aryan, the Semitic and the Turanian,[39] and for each, he sketched a religious typology.[40]

In the reconstruction of the origin of language and thought, Müller gave a central place to the concept of verbal roots.[41] Whatever could not be reduced to a more simple or original form in the words of any language or family of languages he called a root or radical.[42] He regarded these roots as true historical documents which were of major importance for the understanding of the development of the human mind in its early stages. Originally, every root expressed a concept or the consciousness of repeated human acts. When these concepts were applied to objects in nature, a metaphoric extension took place which was characteristic of the early history of religion. It was impossible to express abstract ideas except by metaphor, and it

---

38. Müller 1864, II: 524; 1891, II: 433; Müller 1875, IV: 84 ff.; Müller 1887, 524-525. For a critical evaluation of the 'linguistic paleontology' see, De Saussure 1985: 304 ff. See further Henson 1971 and Stocking 1987: 59-90.
39. Muller reconstructed a common origin for a group of languages such as Turkish, Chinese, Altaic and the like. He called them Turanian but later he regarded this reconstruction as outdated.
40. Müller 1873: 154 ff.
41. For a detailed exposition of his ideas on verbal roots see Müller 1887, especially chapters V-VII.
42. Müller [1861] 1866$^5$, I: 283.

was not too much to say that the whole dictionary of ancient religion was made up of metaphors.[43] In this context, Müller introduced the idea of 'the fundamental metaphor.'

> I speak of the fundamental metaphor which makes us conceive and speak of objects as if they were subjects like ourselves. But, strange as this interpretation of the objective world may seem, and marvellous as this universal mythology to which it has led, it was inevitable. As we know one kind of being only, namely that expresses our own acts and our own states, ..., what can we predicate of outward objects except some kind of being like our own, and what language can we apply to them except which we have framed to express our own acts and our own states.[44]

The theory that language was not only a means of communication but also essential for thinking brought Müller in conflict with the evolutionist theories of Darwin and his followers. He claimed a domain for the human mind (Spirit) which was independent of the material world. He objected to the idea of a humanity emerging from the depth of animal brutality with the words: 'language is our Rubicon and no brute will dare to cross it'.[45] Nonetheless, he accepted an idea of evolution within the varieties, but the borders between them remained fixed. He elaborated his ideas on the evolution of humanity in the *Gifford Lectures* which dealt with his philosophy of religion.[46]

Müller's specific concept of language in relation to *ethnos*, 'nation' or 'tribe', brought him in conflict with some 'social

---

43. Müller 1873: 267; 1887: 327-330.
44. Müller 1887: 327.
45. Müller 1866 [1861¹], I: 15, 385 ff., especially 392; *idem* 1887: 177 ff. cf. also *idem* 1892: 186. Müller repeats this adage on many occasions. For his controversy with Darwin, see Van den Bosch 1993a: 107-18, especially note 56.
46. For a summary of his position see the preface of Müller 1893: esp. IX ff. and XVI, as well as 538-42. See also G. Müller 1902, II: 233 ff. and Sharpe 1975: 45.

evolutionists'.[47] He objected to the explanation of myth and custom in certain cultures by reference to analogies in other cultures. According to him, such a method was explaining the unknown by the more unknown, *ignotum per ignotius*.[48] A thorough knowledge of languages was an absolute requisite for an adequate understanding of other cultures.[49] In addition, he criticized the evolutionistic idea that fetishism and other forms of primitive religion belonged to the earliest strata of religion of mankind. He carefully analysed the concept of fetishism and similar concepts used by ethnologists and claimed that primitive people, like the negroes of West Africa, had a history as long as other people, but it could no longer be reconstructed because of the absence of documents.[50]

With his linguistic and historical approach to religion and its basic concepts,[51] Müller took a relativistic point of view.[52] Moreover, on account of methodological considerations, he restricted his comparisons of religious concepts to those cultures which had a common linguistic heritage. He looked for their common etymology in order to elucidate their original meaning, but he acknowledged the possibility of broader comparisons with respect to cultures with a common linguistic heritage, as proclaimed by the analogical school. During the last decade of his life he became more open to the ethnological or ethno-psychological method.

---

47. Müller refers in various publications to social philosophers and scholars as A. Comte, H. Spencer, J. Lubbock and E. Tylor. For his discussion of the ethnological method see the preface of Müller 1895, IV: esp. XVII-XVIII and XXXV-XLIV. Cf. also Dorson 1968: chapter 6, esp. 187-91 and Stocking 1987: 61 f.; 305-7.
48. Müller 1889: 499; *idem* 1895, IV: pp. XXXV ff.; *idem* 1897, I: 5, 23 f., 28, 128 etc.
49. So e.g. Müller 1895, IV: pp. XXVII ff.; *idem* 1897, I: 177 ff.
50. Müller 1878: 54 ff.; *idem* 1897, I: 194 ff.
51. See Müller 1864: 424: 'The history of religion is in one sense a history of language'.
52. Müller 1873: 261.

## 3. Mythology

Müller was thoroughly influenced by the Romantic movement in his study of mythology.[53] F. Schlegel – with 'Sprache und Weisheit der Inder' (1808) – and Schelling were among the first authors in Germany who in their imagination exalted the Orient for its wisdom. They associated myth with poetry as well as with mankind in its natural state.[54] It was suggested that myth, like 'nature-poetry', originated in the collective unknown and was a product of divine nature which revealed itself in myth. As a collection of the most ancient poetical texts of mankind, with its many references to nature and myth, the *Rigveda* proved an important source for the scientific elaboration of these ideas.[55] For this reason, Müller regarded the comparative study of ancient Aryan mythology as the best preparation for a more comprehensive study of the mythology of other nations and languages.[56] He added to this view:

> I have learnt to appreciate poetical and literary productions as an essential element in mythology and to draw and utilise the consequences arising from this state of things. But on the other hand, I hold it as quite certain that a portion of these older myths arose from nature-poetry which is no longer intelligible to us, but has to be interpreted by means of analogies.[57]

---

53. For a short survey of his ideas on mythology see e.g. Lang 1884: 137-142; Chantepie de la Saussaye 1885: 213-242; Jordan 1905: 294 ff.; Dorson 1965: 25-63; Sharpe 1975: 35 ff.; Neufeldt 1980: 62-92; Turner 1981: 104-115; Stocking 1987: 60-62, 121 and 306; Kippenberg 1997:66-9.
54. See Hofmeister 1978: 102, 124-5 who refers to the famous expression of F. Schlegel in his 'Rede über die Mythologie' (1800): 'Im Oriënt müssen wir das höchste Romantische suchen.' For Schelling's speculations on ancient mythology, see his book: *Über Mythen, historischen Sagen und Philosopheme der ältesten Welt* (1793).
55. See also Neufeldt 1980: 62, 80-7.
56. See Müller 1894-5, II: 75: 'The mythology of the Veda is to comparative mythology what Sanskrit has been to comparative grammar.'
57. Müller 1897, I: preface p. XVII.

With these mythological interpretations, based on analogy with natural phenomena, Müller left his mark on scientific discourse about myth in the second half of the nineteenth century. His principal aim was to discover the central thought underlying every myth or, to put it in his words, 'to discover the reason behind the unreason of mythology' because the bizarre myths called for a scientific explanation.[58] In this context he asked himself:

> Is the whole of mythology an invention, the fanciful poetry of a Homer or Hesiod, or is it a growth? ... Was mythology a mere accident, or was it inevitable? Was it a false step? Or was it a step that could not be left out in the historical progress of the human mind?[59]

Müller tried to find a solution for these questions by means of the etymological method that was developed by comparative philology.[60] He was convinced that the study of the origin and development of words formed its best foundation. From this point of view, he tried to reconstruct common mythical traditions by identifying the names of the principal actors in the myths of ancient Indo-European people. He referred in this context to Vedic mythology, because this represented mythology in a state of fermentation, while other mythologies had already passed through this state.[61] As such, the hymns of the Rigveda contained traces of the earliest periods of mankind, in which the

---

58. Müller 1873: 335-403 (lecture delivered in 1871). For a short description of his later position, see Müller's preface to his second edition of vol. IV of the *Chips from a German Workshop* of 1895, p. XLI ff. An elaborate description and evaluation of the various mythological schools is presented in Müller 1897, I: chapters 2, 3 and 4. See also Dorson 1968: 161 ff.
59. Müller 1873: 352-3.
60. See Müller 1856, reprinted in Müller 1894-5, IV: 17 f., 90 f., 151. See also Müller 1894- 5, IV: preface, pp. XVII-XVII and 378 ff.; *idem* 1897, I: 13 and 21. Cf. Neufeldt 1980: 77-80.
61. See e.g. Müller 1894-5, IV: 332 f; *idem* 1889: 2, 19, 85, etc.; *idem* 1897, I: 13.

concepts of gods and myths were coined.[62] With the etymological method, Müller 'revealed' the deeper meaning of myth and showed that, originally, a fixed symbolic order lay beneath its chaotic surface. This order referred to the great regular phenomena of nature: day and night, sun and moon, the sky, and the like.[63] Early mankind selected these symbols to express sacred reality because regularity in nature would have been especially suggestive of order. This idea was based on his claim that regularity, not the exceptional, induced linguistic incorporation.[64]

Müller regarded a myth as an inevitable byproduct in the development of language and introduced the controversial expression 'disease of language' as the origin of mythology.[65] With this expression he pointed to a development whereby 'language was forgetting itself' and *nomina* became *numina*.[66] This process was regarded by him as the death of symbolism. Whenever a word that was first used metaphorically was used without a clear conception of the steps that led from its original to the metaphorical meaning, mythology was quite possibly present. Whenever those steps were forgotten and other steps artificially put in what we ended up with was mythology.[67] The close relation between the fundamental metaphor and mythology was described by him with the following words:

---

62. Müller 1856, republished in 1894-5, IV: 62 ff.; *idem* 1891b, II: 454 ff. See also Dorson 1968: 162-3.
63. Müller 1856, republished in 1894-5, IV: 90 ff. and 153; *idem* 1864: especially 518; *idem* 1883: 179, 197-8; *idem* 1887: 299; *idem* 1895, IV: p. XII (preface); *idem* 1897, I: 34.
64. Müller 1891b, II: 368; *idem* 1887: 219: 'Every root expresses a concept, or what is called a general notion, or what is more correctly the *consciousness of repeated acts*.' Cf. also Crick 1976: 32.
65. See e.g. Müller 1856, republished in 1894-5, IV: 13 and 56; *idem* 1892 [1891a]: 269-71; *idem* 1891b, I: 11 and II: 452-3, 456; *idem* 1897, I: 68 ff. See also De Vries 1967: 89-90; Neufeldt 1980: 64-6; 74-5; Kitagawa and Strong 1985: 199 ff.; Camporesi 1989.
66. Müller 1894-5, IV [1856]: 13 and 56; *idem* 1873: 278 f.; *idem* 1897, I: 68 ff.
67. Müller 1897, I: 37-8; Cf. also Crick 1976: 29.

> Here is the true riddle of mythology, and, in one sense, of theology also, namely the inevitable metaphor or transference of the subjective to the objective ... The same people who had learnt to speak of themselves as runners now spoke of rivers as runners.[68]

The process of the formation of myths was illustrated by means of natural phenomena, e.g. the sun and the moon, which could be denoted by certain of their characteristic features. This was called *polyonymy* and regarded by Müller as an essential feature of ancient language. In addition, he used the terms *homonymy* or *synonymy* to indicate that the same words could be used for several objects on account of shared characteristics.[69] When the metaphoric character of the language with which the numinal reality in nature was denoted was forgotten, the *nomina* became *numina*. The bright sky as a symbol for the 'Infinite' became the god of heaven, Dyaus, and a new mythology was created which was based on his most important emblems.[70]

Müller dealt with mythology in the context of the science of language but also within the context of the science of thought. He stated that words constantly reacted to our thoughts, and moulded them, or even restrained and fettered them. He especially drew attention to the influence of old and petrified expressions on new living thought. Mythology was in his opinion, in fact, the dark shadow which language threw over thought, and which could never disappear unless language became altogether commensurable with thought, which it never would.[71] From this point of view, the history of philosophy, from Thales to Hegel, was an uninterrupted battle against mythology, a constant protest of thought against language.[72]

---

68. Müller 1887: 328.
69. Müller 1873: 276-7; 1891b, II: 453 ff.; 1897, I: 115.
70. For criticism, see e.g. De Vries 1967: 89.
71. Müller 1867-75, II: 162; *idem* 1873: 353-4.
72. Müller 1873: 355.

Müller formulated the results of his contributions to the science of mythology in his publication of 1897 and stated that:

1) the different branches of Aryan family of speech possessed before their separation not only common words (*mythoi*), but likewise common myths (*mythoi*);
2) what we call the gods of mythology were chiefly the agents supposed to exist behind the great phenomena of nature;
3) the names of some of these gods and heroes, common to some or all branches of the Aryan family of speech, and therefore much older than the Vedic and Homeric periods, constitute the most ancient and most important material on which the students of mythology have to work;
4) the best solvent of the old riddles of mythology is to be found in an etymological analysis of the names of the gods and goddesses and heroes and heroines.[73]

In spite of these results, comparative mythology took a different course.

## 4. Science of Religion

Müller is nowadays regarded as one of the founding fathers of the science of religion together with the Dutch scholar C.P. Tiele.[74] He gave a first impulse to the comparative study of religions and formulated its basic principles in his *Introduction to the Science of Religion*:

---

73. Müller 1897, I: 21.
74. See e.g. Jordan 1905: 161 ff., 521 ff.; Sharpe 1975: 38-39; Trompf 1978; Neufeldt 1980: 92-122; Kitagawa and Strong 1985: 179-213; Kippenberg 1997: 60-79; Klimkeit 1997: 29-41.

> He (the student of religion) wants to find out what Religion is, what foundation it has in the soul of man, and what laws it follows in its historical growth.[75]

Müller stated that a science of religion should be based on an impartial and truly scientific comparison of all, or, at all events, of the most important religions of mankind. Moreover, the method should be critical with respect to the texts and these should be studied in their original language. Though he acknowledged that a distinction should be made between older and younger traditions, he argued that the student of religion should be aware of the continuity between the past and the present.[76]

Classification and comparison of religious concepts were important means in achieving a better understanding of the origin and development of religion.[77] In this context Müller stated that he who knows one religion, knows none, thus paraphrasing a well-known maxim of Goethe.[78] However, these comparisons should not be based on theological arguments, but on the principles of classification from comparative philology.[79] With this view, Müller followed in the footsteps of Herder and W. von Humboldt and accepted the supposed close relationship between language, religion and *ethnos* (national character) for the early history of mankind. By means of comparison and reconstruction within well defined linguistic boundaries, he tried to trace the historical origins of the Aryan, the Semitic, and Turanian religion. The manifestation of God in nature was the most

---

75. Müller 1873: 9. Cf. also Müller 1878: 224-225: 'What we want to know is, how religion is possible; how human beings, such as we are, came to have any religion at all; what religion is, and how it came to be what it is.'
76. Müller, 1873: 22 ff., 34-5.
77. Müller 1873: 122-3.
78. Müller 1873: 15; see also 122-3. Goethe: 'He who knows one language, knows none'.
79. Müller 1873: 143.

important feature of the religion of the Indo-European people, while the manifestation of God in history was essential for the religion of the Semitic people.[80]

One of the central problems Müller dealt with in his Science of Religion and later works was how to define religion. He distinguished two aspects, namely the historical and the psychological. The historical aspect concerned religion as a traditional doctrinal system which was handed down in books, doctrines, rituals, etc. This could be studied by the historian of religion, but religion also had a psychological aspect and this was described by him as a human faculty for faith.[81] Müller distinguished two domains which corresponded with these two aspects, namely the 'Comparative Theology', devoted to the comparative study of religion, and the 'Theoretic Theology', dealing with the philosophy of religion. Religion was initially defined by Müller as a mental faculty:

> a mental faculty or disposition, which independent of, nay, in spite of sense and reason, enables man to apprehend the Infinite under different names and under different disguises.[82]

Müller claimed that comparative theology was the basis of his definition of religion, but in reality the definition rested chiefly on the philosophical discourse of religion among Romantic philosophers, i.e. theologians, as, for instance, Schleiermacher and Schopenhauer. He heavily stressed its psychological aspects and even stated that 'as there is a faculty of speech, independent of all forms of language, so there is a faculty of faith in man, independent of all religions. Without that faculty no

---

80. Müller 1873: 29 and 215-6. For his reconstruction of the Semitic religion see also Olender 1992: 84-5. Müller acknowledged in the last part of his life that his views on the Turanian languages were outdated.
81. Müller 1873: 17; *idem* 1878: 22-3; *idem* 1889: chapters 2-5.
82. Müller 1873: 17.

religion is possible'.[83] This faculty of faith was connected by him with the notion of Infinity or the Beyond. He maintained that Infinity was implicitly given with the sensual perceptions of the finite and present in all historical forms of religion,[84] though he acknowledged that in many cases no word was found for it.[85] For all that, the idea could already be traced in ancient Vedic texts, where it was symbolized in the great phenomena of nature such as fire, water, sun, moon, heaven and earth. For the most ancient period of religion he mentioned in this context:

> The brilliant sky ... was the only unchanging and infinite being that has received a name, and could as yet lend its name to that as yet unborn idea of the Infinite, which disquieted the human mind.[86]

Müller's conception of religion as a 'faculty' of faith was based on the analogy of a 'faculty' of speech. Nonetheless, it was not without problems. For this reason Müller had to specify the notion of faculty as a 'subjective faculty for the apprehension of the Infinite'.[87] In his later definition, he no longer mentioned

---

83. Müller 1873: 12 and 17; *idem* 1878: 22 f. Cf. Müller 1864: 436 where he introduces the idea of a *sensus numinis* as the source of all religion: '... for it is a *sensus* – an immediate perception, not the result of reasoning or generalizing, but an intuition as irresistible as the impressions of our senses. In receiving it we are passive, as least as passive as in receiving from above the image of the sun, or any other impression of the senses, whereas in our reasoning processes we are active rather than passive. This *sensus numinis*, or, as we may call it in more homely language, *faith*, is the source of all religion; it is that without which no religion, whether true or false, is possible.'
84. Müller 1878: 227; 'I tried to show that beyond, behind, beneath and within the finite, the infinite is always present to our senses.' See also *idem* 1883: 175, 201 ff. and Rohl 1985: 1-24.
85. Müller 1878: 45.
86. Müller 1873: 272.
87. Müller 1878: 23-24. He qualifies his concept of faculty as 'a mode of action', never a substantial thing.

the faculty of faith and acknowledged that all (religious) knowledge passed through two gates, the gate of the senses and the gate of reason.[88] With this adaptation he also shaded his notion of the Infinite, as may be clear from the following quotation:

> I felt it incumbent upon me to show how the presentiment of the Infinite rests on the sentiment of the finite and has its real roots in the real, though not yet fully apprehended presence of the Infinite in all our sensuous perceptions of the finite.[89]

Nonetheless, the vague notion of Infinity as the foundation of religion remained disappointing and asked for further precision.[90] In the *Gifford Lectures*, Müller acknowledged this and limited his notion of the infinite to those manifestations which influenced the moral character of man. In this respect, he showed his dependency on Kant's *Critique of Practical Reason* and his new definition of religion ran as follows:

> Religion consists in the perception of the Infinite under such manifestations as are able to influence the moral character of man.[91]

The introduction of the notion of morality in relation to Infinity was not elaborated by Müller in his philosophy of religion and remained problematic. This problem was inherent to Müller's individualistic point of departure which did not take the social dimension of religion into account.

---

88. Müller 1878: 26 ff.
89. Müller 1878: 45.
90. See also Chantepie de la Saussaye 1891: 271 ff.
91. Müller 1989: chapter 7, (Germ ed. 1890, especially 181 f.). Cf. Sharpe 1975: 38-9.

## 5. Evolutionistic views on religion

As the title of his *Hibbert Lectures* shows, Müller was influenced by the evolutionistic ideas of his time and strongly interested in the origin and development of religion, but he did not share the evolutionistic scheme of the ethnologists.[92] He traced the development of ancient Indian religion through its various stages and claimed that it was possible to discover the ancient road on which the Aryans proceeded from the visible to the invisible, from the finite to the Infinite.[93] This earliest period was also described by him metaphorically as the 'childhood of the human race' and its religious language was, then, viewed as the *'parler enfantin'*. Müller regarded the early Vedic religion as a clear example of the 'childhood' of religion.[94] He evoked this stage with the following words:

> If the ancient Greeks or Aryans of India began to ask, whence came the rain and lightning, whence sprang hail and snow, heat and cold, day and night, coming and going in regular and irregular succession, they could only speak of agents and workers, as they spoke of agents and workers who had ploughed the land, forged the iron, or built a hut. And this arose not only from a necessity of thought, but at the same time from a necessity of language. If they wished to form the first names for the wind, or the fire, or the sun by names such as alone their language could produce, they had to make use of the same elements from which all their words had been derived, i.e. the so-called roots, their earliest predicates, their earliest abstractions, their earliest general terms.[95]

---

92. Müller 1878: 219, 363 ff.
93. Müller 1878: 220-2.
94. Müller 1873: 274-5, 279; idem 1878: 370. Cf. also idem 1883: 107 ff.
95. Müller 1897, I: 112-3.

For Müller, this concept of the 'childhood' of religion did not imply a value judgement because the possibilities for the expression of religious truths were restricted by the possibilities of language. For this reason he took a relativistic point of view and described his position as follows:

> When we try to reach the Infinite and the Divine by means of more abstract terms, are we now better than children trying to place a ladder against the sky?[96]

Müller elaborated his evolutionistic ideas into a philosophy of religion in his *Gifford Lectures* and stated that the history of ancient religions clearly showed the 'divine education of the human race'.[97] History teaches us that religions change, and must change, with the constant changes of thought and language in the progress of the human race.[98] In addition to this, he sometimes reversed this perspective and formulated Romantic notions on the origin of religion.

> The more we go back, the more we examine the earliest germs of every religion, the purer, in one sense, shall we find the conceptions of the deity, the nobler the purpose of each founder of a new worship.[99]

From this point of view, the adaption of the pure ideal to concrete reality of everyday life implied a decay. For this very reason, he argued strongly in favour of fair comparisons and he described his own ideas with respect to the comparative study of religion as follows:

---

96. Müller 1873: 279; cf. also p. 261.
97. Müller 1873: 226.
98. Müller 1889: 275. Cf. also 1883: 16 f.
99. Müller 1891b, II: 536.

> The more I study heathen religions, the more I feel convinced that, if we want to form a true judgement of their purpose, we must measure them, as we measure the Alps, by the highest point which they have reached.[100]

Müller often applied notions of childhood, manhood and old age to the evolution of religion and presupposed that metaphors such as organic growth and decay could be applied to religious thought. As such, he also spoke about the dialectic life of religion and associated these processes with the specific character of religious language and thinking.[101] He was convinced that new religious expressions were coined with the evolution of mankind. He traced a development in which the highest goal of religion was described as the yearning for a mystical union or unity with God.

> However imperfect the forms may be in which that human yearning for God has found expression in different religions, it has always been the deepest spring of all religion, and the highest summit reached by Natural Religion.[102]

## 6. Critical Notions and Evaluation

The theories of Max Müller on language, religion, and mythology have been severely criticised. Especially his accentuation of the relationship between language and religion, i.e. mythology, was not generally accepted.[103] Tiele referred in this context to the linguist and indologist W.D. Whitney, a furious opponent of Müller, and objected to the idea that religion could be reduced to 'a sacred dialect of human speech'; religion also implied reli-

---

100. Müller 1878: 108.
101. Müller 1873: 274-7. Cf. also Voigt 1967: 18.
102. Müller 1893: 541-2.
103. For the discussion of Müller's thesis of the 'disease of language', in which the *numina* became *nomina*, see De Vries 1967: 89; Kitagawa and Strong 1985: 199-204.

gious actions which were essential to religious communities.[104] Nonetheless, the relationship between language and thought, i.e. religious concepts, has been an important issue in anthropological discussions until now. E. Sapir, linguist and anthropologist, also relied on Herder and stated that 'language and our thought-grooves are inexplicably interwoven, and are, in a sense, one and the same'.[105] Similar ideas were expressed by his pupil B.L. Whorf and incorporated in the so-called Sapir-Whorf hypothesis, which states that the very structure of language moulds the way in which people conceive of the world in which they find themselves.[106] For this reason, we may observe that Müller in his description and elaboration of linguistic processes in some respects reminds one of modern linguistic philosophy.[107] The idea that man can be misled by language when he no longer understands the original meanings of words and for that reason becomes 'bewitched' is also expressed in modern linguistic philosophy, *inter alia*, in the later work of Wittgenstein.[108]

A second objection concerned Müller's comparative method for the science of religion which was essentially based on linguistic criteria. Religions were classified, analysed, and compared according to linguistic points of view in order to reconstruct their common past.[109] Also, Müller was mainly interested in mythology and only dealt with those materials which originally belonged to the same linguistic family, but his etymological method, which intended to identify the original meaning of names as a clue for the solution of many riddles in mythology and

---

104. Tiele 1871: 98-128. For a critical evaluation of the ideas of F. Max Müller, see also Whitney 1892. For a recent plea to study religion in close connection with language, as had been done by Müller, see Staal 1986: 40.
105. Sapir 1949: 232. Cf. also Sapir 1984: 387 ff. For a recent study on Sapir, see Darnell 1990.
106. Whorf 1956. Cf. also Lyons 1981: 301-12.
107. See also Crick 1976: 30.
108. See Crick 1976: 30. For a critical evaluation of Wittgenstein's ideas, see Gellner 1979.
109. Cf. Chantepie de la Saussaye 1897: 271-91.

religion, led to highly controversial results among the linguists themselves and to many diverging opinions among the representatives of the school of nature-myths.[110] A. Lang was one of the first authors who drew attention to many flaws in the theories of Müller: the evidence was inadequate, the analysis insufficient, and the results too speculative.[111] In a later review the main failures of Müller's theories on mythology were summarised by Chase. This concerned Müller's idea of decay (or degradation), which was implicitly based on Christian presuppositions. Chase also stated that:

> too much emphasis was placed on language and linguistic processes and too little upon differential effects of the social, cultural and physical setting wherein myths originated; and moreover, there was too little concern with origins and not enough with historical development of myth and myth-making.[112]

All these objections are correct, but they do not allow for the fact that Müller had a sharp eye for the symbolic dimension of language which also made itself felt in his theories on religion. Müller never suggested that God was identified with the sun or the moon, nor that metaphorical or poetical language would lead to personification of natural objects.[113] He was of the opinion that primitive man in his orientation on nature used material or natural symbols to interpret his reality because abstract words simply failed. This approach showed the affinity of Max Müller with the 'concrete logic' of 'primitive' and ancient peoples to which Lévi-Strauss has also pointed.[114]

---

110. See e.g. Chase 1949: 47 ff.; De Vries 1967: 187 ff.; Littleton 1973: 33 ff.
111. Lang 1884: 135-57. For Lang's position in relation to Müller, see also Dorson 1968: 170 ff., 206 ff.
112. Chase 1949: 48.
113. This was wrongfully attributed to Müller by Bianchi 1975: 63. Cf. Henson 1974: 38 f.; Crick 1976: 22 f.
114. See e.g. Crick 1976: 24.

Müller's definition of religion and its implications were highly controversial as well. Chantepie de la Saussaye mentioned, for instance, that Müller's definition was one-sided, to say the least; it was founded on the individual and did not take into account the social dimension of religion.[115] Though Müller claimed that his definition was based on the religious materials collected by himself, it was highly abstract and primarily functioned in discussions in the field of the philosophy of religion. De Vries blamed Müller for his lack of psychological understanding and added that 'only accurate observation of primitive religious life leads to valuable insights.'[116]

Notwithstanding these severe criticisms, Müller's contributions to the science of religion have been of paramount importance. He was one of the first scholars who laid the foundations of the science of religion and promoted its development. By lecturing publicly, he presented the new discipline not only to a small group of scholars but also to a wider public and fostered their goodwill. His publications stimulated many contemporary scholars though the comparative research on religion has developed in a different direction. Nonetheless, Müller was honoured by some scholars with the title of 'father' or 'founder' of the science of religion.[117] This was of little significance for Müller, because he, himself, realised that

> it is the fate of all pioneers, not only to be left behind in the assault which they planned, but that many of their approaches were made in the false direction and had to be abandoned.[118]

---

115. Chantepie de la Saussaye 1891: 271 ff.
116. De Vries 1967: 89. Cf. also Evans-Pritchard 1981: 185 f.
117. Cf. Jordan 1905: 150 ff., 521 ff.; Waardenburg 1973, I: 13 f.; Sharpe 1975: 45.
118. Müller 1873: 292.

## Bibliography

Berkenkopf, P. 1914. *Die Voraussetzungen der Religionsphilosophie Friedrich Max Müllers.* Langensalza.
Bianchi, U. 1975. *The History of Religions,* Leiden.
Bopp, F. 1816. *Das Conjugationssystem,* Frankfurt
–. 1845-54. *A Comparative Grammar of Sanskrit, Zend, Greek, Latin, Lithuanian, Gotic, German and Slavonic Languages.* Translated by Lieutenant Eastwick and conducted through the press by H.H. Wilson. 3 vols. London (orig. German ed. Berlin 1833-1852).
Bosch, L.P. van den. 1993a. 'Friedrich Max Müller: Een Victoriaans geleerde over de oorsprong van de taal en het religieuze denken.' *Nederlands Theologisch Tijdschrift* 47 (2): 107-18.
–. 1993b. 'Friedrich Max Müller: Een Victoriaans geleerde over het onderzoek naar mythen en religie.' *Nederlands Theologisch Tijdschrift* 47 (3): 186-200.
–. 1998. 'Theosophy or Pantheism. Friedrich Max Müller's Gifford Lectures on Natural Religion'. In Barlingay, S.S., *Samanvaya (Quest for Harmony),* Pune, pp. 175-215.
Camporesi, Chr. 1989. *Max Müller, la malattia del linguaggio et la malattia del pensiero.* Firenze.
Chantepie de la Saussaye, P.D. 1885. 'Mythologie en Folklore.' *De Gids* 15: 213-42.
–. 1891. 'Max Müller als Gifford Lecturer.' *De Gids* 21: 271-92.
Chase, R. 1949. *The Quest for Myth,* Baton Rouge.
Chaudhuri, N.C. 1974. *Scholar Extraordinary, The Life of Professor Rt. Hon. Friedrich Max Müller P.C.* London.
Crick, M 1976. *Explorations in Language and Meaning: Towards a Semantic Anthropology.* London.
Darnell, R. 1990. *Edward Sapir, Linguist, Anthropologist, Humanist.* Berkeley.
Dorson, R.M. 1965. 'The Eclipse of Solar Mythology.' In T.A. Sebeok, ed., *Myth: a Symposium.* London.
–. 1968. *The British Folklorists: a History.* London.
Evans-Pritchard, E.E. 1981. *A History of Anthropological Thought.* London and Boston.
Frei, H. 1985. 'David Friedrich Strauss.' In N. Smart, J. Clayton, S. Katz, P. Sherry, eds., *Nineteenth Century Religious Thought in the West.* Vol. I. Cambridge.
Grimm, J. 1819-1837. *Geschichte der Deutschen Sprache.* Berlin.
Henson, H. 1971. 'Early British Anthropologists and Language.' In E. Ardener, ed., *Social Anthropologists and Language.* London.
–. 1974. *The British Social Anthropologists and Language: A History of Seperate Development.* London.
Herder, J.G. 1895 (1770[1]). *Abhandlung über den Ursprung der Sprache.* Ed. B. Suphan, vol. V, Berlin.

Hofmeister, G. 1978. *Deutsche und europäische Romantik.* Stuttgart.
Jankowski, K.R. 1979. 'F. Max Müller and the Development of Linguistic Science.' *Historio graphica Linguistica* 6: 346 ff.
Jordan, L.H.J. 1905. *Comparative Religion: Its Genesis and Growth.* Edinburgh (repr. Atlanta 1986).
Kippenberg, H.G., 1997. *Die Entdeckung der Religionsgeschichte. Religionswissenschaft und Moderne.* München.
Kitagawa, J.M. and Strong, J.S. 1985. 'Friedrich Max Müller and the Comparative Study of Religion.' In N. Smart, J. Clayton, S. Katz and P Sherry, eds., *Nineteenth Century Religious Thought in the West.* Vol. III. Cambridge.
Klimkeit, H.J., 1997. 'Friedrich Max Müller'. In A. Michaels (ed.), *Klassiker der Religionswissenschaft.* München.
Lang, A. 1884. 'Mythology.' *Encyclopaedia Britannica* (ninth ed.). Vol. XVII, pp. 135-57.
–. 1900. 'Obituary on Max Müller.' *Contemporary Review* (London) 78: 784-93.
Lyons, J. 1981. *Language and Linguistics.* London.
Moncalm, M. 1900. *L'Origine de la pensée et de la parole.* Paris.
Morgan, R. 1985. 'Ferdinand Christian Baur.' In N. Smart, J. Clayton, S. Katz and P Sherry, eds., *Nineteenth Century Religious Thought in the West.* Vol. I. Cambridge.
Max Müller, F. 1849-74. *Rigveda and Sāyana's Commentary.* 6 vols. Oxford.
–. 1856. *Essay on Comparative Religion.* London (republ. in *Chips*, II (1868), 1-146 and *Chips* IV ($1895^2$), 1-154).
–. 1859. *A History of Ancient Sanskrit Literature.* London (repr. Varanasi 1968).
–. [1861] *Lectures on the Science of Language.* I. London (1866 $^{5\,\text{rev.\,ed.}}$).
–. 1864. *Lectures on the Science of Language.* II. London.
–. 1867-75$^1$. *Chips from a German workshop.* London (5 vols: 1867, I; 1868, II; 1870, III; 1875, IV and V).
–. 1873. *Introduction to the Science of Religion.* London (repr. New York 1978).
–. 1878. *Lectures on the Origin and Growth of Religion, as Illustrated by the Religions of India.* London (repr. New York 1987).
–. 1881. *Immanuel Kant's Critique of Pure Reason: In Commemoration of the Centennary of its First Publication.* With an introduction by L. Noiré. London.
–. 1883. *India, What Can It Teach Us?.* London.
–. 1887. *The Science of Thought.* London.
–. 1889. [1890*] *Natural Religion.* London (German ed. *Natürliche Religion.* Leipzig 1890*).
–. 1891a. [1892*] *Physical Religion.* London (German ed. *Physische Religion.* Leipzig 1892*).
–. 1891b. *The Science of Language: Founded on the lectures delivered at the Royal Institution.* 2 vols. London (thoroughly revised edition with a new preface).
–. 1892. [1893*] *Anthropological Religion.* London (German ed. *Anthropologische Religion.* Leipzig 1893*).

—. 1893. *Theosophy or Psychological Religion.* London.
—. 1894-5². *Chips from a German Workshop.* 5 vols. London (a totally revised and expanded edition with new articles and many changes).
—. 1897. *Contributions to the Science of Mythology.* 2 vols. London.
—. 1898a. *Rāmakrishna: His Life and Sayings.* London.
—. 1898-9b. *Auld Lang Syne.* 2 vols. London.
—. 1899a. *The Six Systems of Indian Philosophy.* London.
—. 1901a. *My Autobiography: A Fragment.* London (repr. New York 1909).
—. 1901b. *Last Essays.* London.
Max Müller, G., ed. 1902. *The Life and Letters of the Right Honorable Friedrich Max Müller.* 2 vols. New York, London and Bombay.
Neufeldt, R.W. 1980. *F. Max Müller and the Rigveda: A study of its role in his work and thought.* Calcutta.
Olender, M. 1992. *The Language of Paradise: Race, Religion and Philology in the Nineteenth Century.* Cambridge (Mass.) and London.
Pater, W. de. 1986. *Filosofie van de Taal.* Leuven.
Rohl, J. 1985. 'Sinn und Geschmack fürs Unendliche.' *Neue Zeitschrift für Systematische Theologie und Religionsphilosophie* 27: 1-24.
Rudolph, K. 1962. *Die Religionsgeschichte an der Leipziger Universität.* Berlin.
Sapir, E. 1949 (1921¹). *Language.* New York.
—. 1984 (1905¹). 'Herder's Ursprung der Sprache.' *Historiographia Linguistica* 2: 387 ff.
de Saussure, F. 1985 (1910-1911¹). *Cours de linguistique générale.* Ed. by T. de Mauro. Paris.
Sharpe, E. 1975. *Comparative Religion: a History.* London.
Staal, F. 1986. 'The Sound of Religion.' *Numen* 33: 33-64, 185-224.
Steinthal, H., 1858², *Der Ursprung der Sprache im Zusammenhang mit den letzten Fragen alles Wissens,* Berlin. (revised and expanded ed. 1877³; and again revised and expanded in 1888⁴).
Stocking, G.W. (jr.). 1987. *Victorian Anthropology.* New York.
Stolz, F. 1988. *Grundzüge der Religionswissenschaft.* Göttingen.
Tiele, C.P. 1871. 'Een Probleem der Godsdienstwetenschap.' *De Gids* 1: 98-128.
Trompf, G. 1978. *Friedrich Max Müller as a Theorist of Comparative Religion.* Bombay.
Turner, F.M. 1981. *The Greek Heritage in Victorian Britain.* New Haven and London.
Vries, J. de. 1967. *The Study of Religion, A Historical Approach.* New York.
Waardenburg, J. 1973. *Classical Approaches to the Study of Religion.* 2 vols. Berlin and The Hague.
Whitney, J.D. 1892. *Max Müller and the Science of Language.* New York.
Whorf, B.L. 1956. *Language, Thought and Reality.* Cambridge (Mass.).

# The History of Religions and the History of Authority

*Bruce Lincoln*
UNIVERSITY OF CHICAGO, USA

I want to talk about three topics today: the history of religions, comparison, and authority. With regard to the first two themes, I will try to be brief, and will speak in terms that are general and schematic, perhaps overly so. With regard to the last, however, I hope to offer a little more concretion and detail.

## History and/of the History of Religions

Let me begin by asserting that history of religions is no longer – if indeed, ever it was – an offshoot of theology, and is no longer – if ever it was – motivated by a desire to explain the ways of god to man. Rather, it is firmly and properly situated within the human sciences, and as such its task is to explicate a critically important dimension of human thought, experience, and expression. It is, in effect, a discourse about that discourse which is religion; alternately, an inquiry into that inquiry which is religion, or a (scholarly) practice effected upon those practices which are religion. But in all these instances, the study remains detached from and independent of that which is studied. Thus, whereas the discourse that constitutes religion is oriented toward the celestial, the transcendent, the divine, and the eternal, that discourse which constitutes the history of religions is – or ought be – unambiguously, unapologetically, and relentlessly oriented toward the contingent, the terrestrial, and the temporal. There is, then, something vaguely ironic about our task, since our object of study appears to be the changing ways in which humans have thought and talked about those things they take to be eternal and unchanging.

If it is our business to be attentive to historic changes, we are obliged to acknowledge the trend that is evident within recent centuries – particularly since the European Enlightenment – for religious discourses and practices to lose ground to those of science, art, literature, psychiatry, law, *et al.*, and for religious institutions to recede in similar fashion before the advance of such rival institutions as schools, universities, museums, publishing houses, film studios, hospitals, courts, charitable foundations, and the state. Given this, it is of more than passing interest to observe the predilection we historians of religions have for studying the religions of antiquity and those of non-European societies, i.e. precisely those contexts in which religious discourses and institutions have not yet ceded their pride of place. Surely this is no accident, and one begins to suspect that our discipline may have positioned itself (consciously or unconsciously) in a stance of implicit protest against the diminishing role and importance of religion in the modern west. Such a stance, however, seems to me unfortunate, not because it misconstrues these historic processes (which are real enough), but because it commits historical research to a project of nostalgia or, worse yet, one of reaction. Clearly, more studies of many sorts are needed if we are going to steer our field in a more critical and progressive direction. Among these are comparative ventures in which data from the post-Enlightenment period play an important role, and in which materials on either side of this temporal divide are treated in an equally critical manner. Before introducing one such study, however, let me first reflect a bit on the nature of comparison.

## Comparing Comparisons

In contrast to those who have become skeptical about the value – or even the possibility – of comparison, I continue to believe that all knowledge originates with and depends upon comparative inquiry. Fish, I would argue, do not begin to know water until they break the surface of their liquid environs and for the first time encounter air. This is to say that the experience of any entity in isolation is sterile and produces neither reflection, nor the capacity for reflection, since that isolate will be taken for granted and mistaken for "nature", i.e. the sole extant possibility, which simply *is* and cannot be otherwise. As such, it will remain virtually invisible and provoke no comment. It is the recognition of other comparable entities that changes this situation, as it throws the no-longer-isolated (and no-longer-naturalized) entity into a relation of contrastive and enlightening relief with the alternate possibilities that emerge in the moment of comparison.

When a fish first meets air, then, knowledge of various sorts becomes possible. Initially, the fish recognizes the difference between two surrounding media, while simultaneously perceiving the different nature of its own relations with and reactions to these media (breathing in one, choking in the other). Others, whose position lets them observe a variety of creatures, both in the water and out, may also come to understand by virtue of comparison that mammals breathe in air and choke in water, while with fish it is just the reverse, and that an intermediate class of amphibians is able to breathe in both. Given sufficient curiosity, ingenuity, and the right kind of tools – x-rays, dissection equipment, etc. – they can work out an explanatory account in which the differential responses of different species to different environments are shown to result from their possessing different organic structures: lungs, gills, or both.

Although this is no doubt obvious, for the sake of clarity it is worth underlining that all the comparisons I have described – and all comparisons in general – involve, at a minimum, three entities: two that are compared, and one that does the comparing. The relations among these three are anything but simple. First, one must always remember that it is the comparer who selects the things compared and brings them together in such a way as to serve his or her purposes. Second, although the comparer may choose to stress resemblances or differences, the relation that obtains between the things compared is one of (perceived) similarity, not identity or absolute discontinuity. And most often it is the resemblances which provide the ground for comparison (air and water are both environmental media; lungs and gills are both organs for obtaining oxygen), and the differences which suggest the purpose of comparing (do lungs or gills work better in water?).

From this example, we can also observe that it is possible to frame a comparison in a variety of ways by changing the level of specificity and generalization at which it is advanced. Thus, one can compare organs (lungs to gills), organisms (fish to mammals), environments (air to water), or even planetary systems of environments (the air and water of Earth as compared to those of Mars). Such changes, however, co-vary with changes in the purpose for which one undertakes the comparison, the types of detailed evidence that have relevance for the inquiry, the degree of specialization that the investigator needs to possess, and also the identity of the audience that may potentially take an interest in the results. As might be expected, different sorts of challenges and opportunities attend comparisons that are pitched at different levels. Comparisons at a low level of generalization, i.e. those drawn between entities that resemble one another strongly and have only subtle differences – the comparison of a salmon's gills to those of a trout, for example – run the risk of pedantry, and normally engage the attention of only a few specialists or enthusiasts. The opposite type of endeavor – i.e. one in which the items compared have strong differences and subtle resemblances (the comparison of plants to animals or Earth to Mars) – runs the risk of banality, and of engaging an audience as shallow as it is broad.

The relevance of these examples may become clear if we consider some of the types of comparison that have been practiced within our discipline, and some of the controversies that have sprung up between those who advocate types of comparison that are pitched at differing levels. Such is evident, for example, in the gentle, but pointed, prefatory remarks which Georges Dumézil contributed to Mircea Eliade's *Traité d'histoire des religions*. Whereas Eliade (like Pettazzoni, van der Leeuw, Frazer, and others before him) sought to explicate religion *per se*, and thus employed comparisons in which data from any part of the globe and any moment in time might legitimately be introduced, Dumézil made clear his preference for focusing more narrowly on the religions of a group of peoples who are closely related to one another. In this stance, he followed others who have undertaken similar projects, either with reference to Indo-European religions (Friedrich Max Müller, Hermann Güntert) or to the religions of other relatively large, but linguistically or spatio-temporally bounded groups, such as those of the Roman Empire or the Ancient Near East (e.g. Angelo Brelich, Henri Frankfort, Heinrich Zimmer, M.J. Vermaseren, Geo Widengren).

As a result, Dumézil drew on a much more restricted body of evidence than did Eliade, while also employing a more rigorous set of methods, and producing results of more interest to specialists and less to the non-scholarly public. Similar issues may be perceived in the critical stance that has been adopted by Jean-Pierre Vernant, Marcel Detienne, and others of their *école* toward those whom they regard as engaging in an irresponsibly wide-ranging comparatism (Walter Burkert, Réné Girard, e.g.). What they voice as a criticism of comparison, however, I believe is better understood as a critique of certain *forms* of comparison, specifically those that are pitched at a more encompassing level than that with which the critics are comfortable. For when one confronts Dionysiac and Pythagorean data, as Vernant and Detienne regularly do, or Homeric texts with those of the Attic tragedies, one is still practicing comparison, albeit a comparison that has as its goal the explication of Greek religion, not that of the Indo-Europeans, still less of religion in general.

## Toward a Comparative History of Authority

As one who studied under Eliade, practiced forms of comparison much like those of Dumézil, and more recently has shifted to a position closer to that of Vernant and Detienne, these issues have real importance for me. For the most part, the intellectual trajectory I have travelled over the course of my career has been one that leads away from comparative ventures pitched at the higher levels of generality toward those at greater levels of specificity. Still, nothing that I have learned has ever led me to renounce the far-ranging endeavors and grand ambitions of comparison on the scale of an Eliade or a Pettazzoni. If one wishes to understand religion *in general* – a goal that still strikes me as worthwhile, if elusive – it remains necessary to compare broadly, so that the religious experience of some select fraction of humanity is not misrepresented as religion *per se*.

Beyond this, I would also maintain that there are places where a comparative enterprise that is even broader still might hold considerable promise. I have already mentioned my desire to see studies that would encompass data from eras both before and after the Enlightenment. Among these, I am particularly interested in some that would juxtapose religious and non-religious materials in such a way as to elucidate not the history of religions, but the history of authority.

Although definitions are always problematic, it is still useful for me to indicate what I mean by authority, if only to make clear how and why I as comparer have selected the examples that follow. Provisionally, then, I would define authority as that X which permits speakers to command not just the attention, but the confidence, respect, and trust of their audiences, (or to make audiences act *as if* this were the case). Beyond this, I would suggest that authority is not so much an entity as it is: 1) an effect that is produced through acts of discourse; 2) the capacity for producing that effect; and 3) the commonly shared opinion that a given actor, group, or institution has the capacity for producing that effect. More precisely, I take this effect to result from the conjuncture of the right speaker, the right speech, the right staging, the right time and the right place in the presence of an audience, whose historically and culturally conditioned expectations establish the parameters of what is judged "right" in all these instances. When these crucial elements of a discursive situation combine in such a way as to produce attitudes of trust, respect, docility, acceptance, even reverence in the audience, "authority" is the result

Turning to specific data, let me begin with a celebrated episode from the *Iliad*, in which Thersites berates Agamemnon and is chastised for this by Odysseus. All action is set in the assembly place (the *agorē*), which elsewhere is called the "sacred circle" (*hieros kyklos*, *Iliad* 18.504), in which participants met to discuss the most serious of issues. Participants, however, came in two forms. On the one hand, there were those of high rank, who sat closest to the center on a ring of stones, while further from the center others sat on the ground and participated less fully in the proceedings.

Although the Homeric texts do not include anything like a copy of their Rules of Order, we may still infer the standard practices by noting the patterns and regularities that recur in the numerous descriptions of assemblies. Generally, an assembly was called by a sovereign king or high-ranking hero, who sent out his heralds to announce the meeting and to bring others to the assembly-place. Once gathered, people took their seats, and the person who called the meeting would speak first and explain his purposes, after which others might follow. To address the group, one rose from his seat and stepped into the center, after receiving a sceptre from one of the heralds. This sceptre served as the tangible token of one's right to stand, enter, and speak in this setting. With one exception only, all those who held forth in the center of the assembly did so with sceptre in hand, and with the same exception, all held the rank of king (*basileus*).

That exception is found in Book Two of the *Iliad*, a book that is dominated throughout by the image of the sceptre. Thus, immediately upon awaking, Agamemnon dressed himself in royal raiments, taking up last of all "the sceptre of his fathers, ever undecaying" (2.46: *aiei apthiton*). He then convened those described as "sceptre-bearing kings" (2.86: *skēptoukhoi basilēes*) in a small council (a *boulē*), where he explained his plan to test the troops by calling a general assembly (an *agorē*), in which he would disingenuously offer them the opportunity to go home. We then see Agamemnon rising to speak at the start of that assembly, with sceptre in hand (2.100-101), at which point the text

47

pauses to recount how that sceptre was made by Hephaestus for Zeus, how Zeus had Hermes deliver it to Pelops, and how it descended from Pelops through the line of Argive kings down to Agamemnon (2.101-108).

A sacred history is thus provided for the sceptre, a history that describes its divine origin and traces its transmission through a line of illustrious rulers, such that the sceptre comes to be understood as bearing the sedimented power of all these kings, as well as Zeus's initial favor, from which all royal power descends. After this brief but significant mythological excursus, the text returns to Agamemnon as he leans on his sceptre, from which he draws physical, as well as ideological support (2.109), as he executes his plan and suggests to the troops that they return home. Contrary to his intentions and hopes, however, the longsuffering soldiers take him seriously: directly they jump to their feet and run for the ships, screaming with joy, and it is only Odysseus's intervention that saves the day. After obtaining the sceptre from Agamemnon (2.186), he uses it as a goad or weapon with which to herd the soldiers back (2.199: note use of the verb *elaunō*), and also as an item of discourse with which to repersuade them of the king's authority and the necessity of kings:

> "In no way do we Achaeans all rule as
>    kings here.
> The leadership of many is no good thing.
>    Let there be one leader,
> One king, *to whom the child of deviously
>    cunning Cronus gave
> The sceptre...*" (2.203-206).

Once back at the assembly, however, it was neither Agamemnon nor Odysseus who rose to speak. Rather, it was a man named Thersites, the sole commoner who is found in the center of the assembly in either of the Homeric poems, and the only person who speaks there without holding in his hands the golden sceptre.

> Then the others sat down, and settled in
>     their seats,
> But still Thersites of the unmeasured words
>     alone scolded.
> He could hurl many words from his heart,
>     disorderly ones,
> Idly and not according to order, to make
>     strife with kings,
> [Saying] anything that he thought might be
>     laughable
> To the Argives. (2.211-216).

As might be expected, this Thersites – whose name marks him as one possessed of great daring or audacity – launches into a denunciation of Agamemnon, accusing him of greed, laziness, lustful desires, exploitation of others, etc., and he raises once again – this time in earnest – the suggestion that the Greeks abandon the war and make sail for home. In all this, Thersites echoes remarks that Achilles made in Book One, where he denounced Agamemnon before the same audience, in the same place and under closely related circumstances, using much more violent language. Yet in contrast to Thersites, Achilles was a king, and he spoke while holding the sceptre (1.234-237; note that he hurls it down at the end of his speech 1.245-246).

By the normal rules and standards of his society, Thersites was out of line. More precisely, he was out of place, and most precisely of all, he was *speaking* out of place. Once again Odysseus set things to rights.

> Looking darkly, Odysseus rebuked him with
>     these harsh words:
> "Thersites, although a clear orator, you
>     are indiscriminate in your speech.
> Desist, and do not have a mind to make
>     strife against kings.
> For I say that there is no one who is
>     lowlier than you

Among those who came with Atreides to
   Troy.
Therefore *you ought not speak in assembly*
   ...
This I say to you – and it will come to
   pass –
If I come upon you acting as senselessly
   as you do now,
No more may the head of Odysseus sit upon
   his shoulders,
And no more may I be known as Telemachus's
   father
If I do not seize you and strip off your
   clothes,
Your cloak and your chiton that cover your
   shameful parts,
And send you weeping to the swift ships,
*Driving you out of the assembly* with
   unseemly blows."
Thus Odysseus spoke, *and he struck him
   with the sceptre*
On the back and shoulders. Thersites
   doubled over, shed a thick tear,
And a bloody welt rose up on his back
Under the golden sceptre. He sat
   down, terrified
And pained, and looking about aimlessly,
   he wiped away the tears. (2.245-269).

Nowhere does Odysseus debate with Thersites or dispute what he says, for the issue is not Thersites' content, but rather his right to speak. Actually, the issue is his right to *agoreuein*, a verb formed from the noun *agorē*, and which means "to speak *in assembly*." It is precisely this which Odysseus would deny Thersites, whom he tells "you ought not speak *in assembly*" (2.250: *ouk... **agoreuois***) and whom he threatens to drive *from the assembly-place* (2.264: *peplēgōn **agorēthen***) should there be any recurrence of his offence. That Thersites may say the very same things at some other time and in some other place is thus implicitly left open, and prior action has shown that a king like Achilles (cf. Diomedes at 9.32-33) can say them within the assembly. It is the appearance of a speaker without a sceptre in the center of the assembly – an unauthorized speaker in the place where speech-acts acquire their authority – that Odysseus judges improper and intolerable, and he makes good his point by a blow that changes Thersites' position in three distinct ways: from center to periphery, standing to sitting, speaking to crying. This blow, fittingly enough, he administers with the sceptre.

These data reveal that within the society described in the Homeric poems, authority (as I have defined it) was a monopoly of the "sceptre-bearing kings." The sceptre they bore was the material representation of their authority, and was represented as a gift from Zeus, that carried with it the bundle of powers and prerogatives that together constitute kingship. Chief of these, as evidenced in the ways the sceptre was used, was privileged access to the center of the assembly, i.e. the place where the most consequential of speech was produced and heard. And should their monopoly be challenged by others seeking access to this place of privileged speech, Homeric kings had sufficient force at their disposal to repel these intruders (usurpers?), and to make of them an object lesson, as becomes evident in Odysseus' treatment of Thersites. Wrapped in gold though it was, the sceptre remained a club, just as power wrapped in legitimacy still remains power (see the physical description of it at 1.234-237 and 245-246).

To this example from the most ancient text of western literature, let me juxtapose another, taken from an Associated Press story that ran in most American newspapers in April 1992. The setting for this story is a palace of sorts: the Las Vegas Hilton, and more specifically the podium which stands at the head of the Hilton's banquet hall. There, tribute in the form of a crystal statue some 75 cm in height and 12 kilos in weight was being paid to a former king. What transpired is reported in the *Minneapolis Star Tribune*:

Las vegas, Nev. April 13 – An Antinuclear activist rushed at former President Ronald Reagan while he was giving a speech Monday, grabbed a large crystal statue and smashed it. Pieces of glass hit Reagan in the head, but he wasn't hurt.

The man then tried to speak into the microphone as Reagan, appearing startled and angry, stood next to him. But Secret Service agents grabbed the protester, shoved him into the podium and tackled him. Reagan, 81, was jostled during the scuffle.

Agents hustled the man away while others rushed Reagan to the side of the stage at the National Association of Broadcasters convention at the Las Vegas Hilton.

Reagan returned to the podium moments later to applause from the audience of several hundred broadcasters. He picked up a piece of the broken statue, which the association had presented to him, and finished his speech.

If Mr. Reagan plays Agamemnon in this drama, the part of Thersites is assumed by one Richard Paul Springer, a forty-one-year-old activist, who had worked for several years to organize "The Hundredth Monkey Project," something he hoped would be a mix of entertainment and politics in the spirit of Woodstock and Live Aid: a massive set of concerts and demonstrations that would bring together groups and individuals committed to peace and the environment, to demand an end to the testing of nuclear weapons. Reality inevitably fell short of this bold vision, as one can imagine, but even so, as a result of his efforts, over the weekend of April 10-12 more than two thousand people gathered out in the desert in the general vicinity of the Nevada Test Site, where they listened to music and speeches, shared ideas, and dramatized their opposition to nuclear tests. The following Monday, many made the trip into Las Vegas to demonstrate at the U.S. Department of Energy, where twenty four of them were arrested.

From there, Springer made his way to the Hilton and his encounter with the former president. What he wanted to say from the podium may never be fully known, but in a general fashion may be inferred from other remarks that he made. Thus, as he rushed toward the podium, he asked Mr. Reagan how he could speak when nuclear weapons were being tested, and as officers of the secret service dragged him away, he could still be heard shouting: "There's a nuclear test Tuesday, tomorrow afternoon." And when, on October 22 he pled guilty to the charge of interfering with the Secret Service, Mr. Springer explained his actions as follows:

> I attended the National Association of Broadcasters Convention, without a concrete plan, but the plan formulated as I was there; and I made a decision that I was willing to take the stage in order to make an announcement about an upcoming nuclear bomb test.... I believe that each nuclear bomb test is actually polluting present and future generations, and I believe that it is – it is the same as calling out to the world that we are about to have a bomb dropped on us, because in essence we are. So with that information I approached the podium to announce to this broadcasters' convention.

I hope I do not have to belabor all of the ways in which these two episodes resemble one another, nor those in which they differ. As always, there are similarities and divergences, the relative importance of which will vary according to the identity of the comparer and the purposes for which she or he compares. If the sole and exclusive concern of a historian of religions is the specifically religious dimension of the two cases, it is here that their differences are most pronounced. For whereas the authority of a Homeric king – as embodied in his sceptre and its attendant mythic narratives – is religiously constituted, that of an American president is not. No one claims that Reagan's crystal statue, his podium, his microphone, or the other instruments through which he commands the respect and attention of his audience came to him by divine agency, and although some deluded few might think otherwise, the foundational documents of American society and most citizens treat the presidential office and its authority as deriving from the will of the people, not that of God. From the specific vantage point of our discipline, the difference between religious and secularly based authorities is virtually absolute, and others, most notably Hannah Arendt, have gone so far as to argue that authority without the support of religion is virtually no authority at all.

If students of religion and those who understand authority primarily in terms of its ideological justifications are likely to accentuate the differences in the Thersites incident and that of Richard Paul Springer, students of social dramas and those who understand authority primarily in terms of its discursive practices will be more inclined to dwell on the similarities. Thus, they will observe that both episodes involve struggles in which the attempt of an unauthorized person to speak in an authorizing place provoked a violent riposte by defenders of the normative order. And one can even find commonalities between the sceptre and the microphone, as has Pierre Bourdieu, who sees in both "the visible manifestation of the hearing granted to the orator, of his credit, of the social importance of his acts and his words."

For me, neither of these positions is totally satisfying, although my sympathies lie much more with Bourdieu than with Arendt (and least of all with those epigones of Arendt who have made it their project to reinvigorate religion in order to reinforce an authority they take to be perpetually in crisis). *Pace* Arendt, I am inclined to think first, that the authority of those who head modern states is no less than that of their ancient and medieval counterparts; second, that authority works similarly whether it is legitimated through a religious ideology or through mystificatory claims of other sorts. Still, it is worth noting that not all claims are equally mystificatory, and it is here that I have some reservations about the position of Bourdieu. For although I would grant that the sceptre and the microphone are similar in the very ways he posits, still I would insist on some differences. For in contrast to the microphone (and most other post-Enlightenment instruments and representations of authority), the sceptre has religious claims inscribed upon it: claims which locate the source of authority outside the human sphere, and which, if accepted, effectively place that authority beyond argument or contestation.

In the preceding discussion, at various moments I have sought to compare two sequences of events, the abstract categories at issue in those events, the relevant historic eras, and also two modes of comparison. Ultimately, I have tried to show that one of these modes, practiced by those who focus exclusively on religion and who understand religion in a relatively conventional sense, will of necessity accentuate the differences in the two episodes, for they differ precisely on the point of religion. The other mode, practiced by those for whom religion is one point of interest among many, will acknowledge the differences between religious and secular modes of legitimation, also between the eras in which one rather than the other tends to predominate, but will stress how similar the operations of authority are, regardless of the legitimating arguments it invokes and on which it depends.

Personally, I favor this latter path for a number of reasons. Not least is my belief that in this way we are most likely to avoid a catastrophic set of mistakes that involves cutting the past off radically from the present, siding with the past against the present, and simultaneously cutting ourselves off from most of our colleagues in the other human sciences. Against this bleak prospect, it is my fervent hope that we can learn to be not only good historians of religions, but also historians of authority, of ideology, of ceremonial, of etiquette, of knowledge and speculation, and much, much more.

# Bibliography

**Sources**

Homer, *The Iliad*, ed. A.T. Murray. Cambridge, Mass: Harvard University Press, 1971.
Homer, *The Odyssey*, ed. A.T. Murray. Cambridge, Mass: Harvard University Press, 1974.
*Minneapolis Star Tribune*, 14 April 1992, p. 7A: "Protester rushes podium as Reagan speaks."
*New York Times*, 14 April 1992, p. A16: "Reagan Unhurt After Man Smashes 30-Pound Statue."
*New York Times*, 16 April 1992, p. A8: "Protester at Reagan Speech Had Press Credentials." United States of Amercia vs. Rick Paul Springer, Las Vegas, Nevada, October 22, 1992 (Docket No. CR-S-92-109-PMP[RJJ]).

**Secondary Literature**

Andreev, Jurij V. 1979. "Die politischen Funktionen der Volksversammlung im homerischen Zeitalter: Zur Frage der 'militärischen Demokratie'." *Klio* 61: 385-405.
Arendt, Hannah. 1958. "What was Authority?" In Carl J. Friedrich, ed., *Authority*. Cambridge, Mass.
Bendix, Reinhard. 1978. *Kings or People: Power and the Mandate to Rule*. Berkeley.
Bourdieu, Pierre. 1991. *Language and Symbolic Power*. Cambridge, Mass.
Cairns, Francis. 1982. "Cleon and Pericles: A Suggestion." *Journal of Hellenic Studies* 102: 203-204.
–. 1978. "Ces religions dont nous heritons: Un dialogue entre Mircea Eliade et Georges Dumézil." *Les nouvelles littéraires* (2 November), pp. 17-18.
Chantraine, Pierre. 1963. "A propos de Thersite." *L'Antiquité classique* 32: 18-27.
Detienne, Marcel. 1979. *Les maitres de vérité dans la grèce archaïque*. Paris.
Donlan, Walter. 1979. "The Structure of Authority in the Iliad." *Arethusa* 12: 51-70.
Dumézil, Georges. 1948. "Préface." In Mircea Eliade, *Traité d'histoire des religions*. Paris.
Finley, M.I. 1979. *The World of Odysseus*, (2nd ed.). Harmondsworth.
Lincoln, Bruce. 1991. *Death, War, and Sacrifice: Studies in Ideology and Practice*. Chicago.
Tambiah, Stanley J. 1984. *The Buddhist Saints of the Forest and the Cult of the Amulets*. Cambridge.
Vernant, Jean-Pierre. 1977. "Inaugural Address at the College de France, 5th December 1975." *Social Science Information* 16: 5-24.
Vlachos, Georges C. 1974. *Les sociétés politiques homériques*. Paris.

# Freyja: The Trivalent Goddess

*Britt-Mari Näsström*
UNIVERSITY OF GOTHENBURG, SWEDEN

In the sources of Old Norse mythology, Freyja is often described as the particular goddess of love and passion. Like her relatives among the Vanir, Njörð and Freyr, she supports fertility in beasts and soil.[1] It seems, however, that her special realm was that of love among mankind and love poetry. Her myths, as well as Skaldic poetry, echo her own love affairs. *Á hana er gott at heita til ásta* "She is good to evoke in love affairs", Snorri Sturlason assumes[2] and he characterises her as *ásta guð* 'the love goddess'.[3] Sensual and adulterous, she was said to be involved in scandalous affairs, even with her own brother. Historians of religions have seen in her "a typical picture of a fertility goddess."[4] Freyja's favourite animal, the cat, reflects her lascivious character, according to G. Turville-Petre.[5] J. de Vries notes that it is quite natural that she is called Sýr 'the sow' as a symbol of unlimited fertility.[6] Although most male gods act polygamously or even rape goddesses and giantesses, it is Freyja always who is charged with unlimited lasciviousness.

---

1. The Vanir constitute together with the Æsir the pantheon of Old Norse Religion. According to Snorri Sturlason, Freyja together with her father Njörð joined the Æsir as hostages after their war with the Vanir (Glf. 23; Hkr. 4). The name Vanir is related to Skr. vanah 'desire' and the Roman Venus.
2. Glf. 24.
3. Sksm. 20.
4. Ström 1963: 101.
5. Turville-Petre 1964: 176.
6. de Vries 1970 II: 313. This appellation rather means 'protectress', a more fitting name of the goddess than the plump 'mother-sow'. It is true that Freyja's mount is a boar, Hildisvíni, 'war boar' in Hdl. 7.

Indeed, she behaves very wickedly in some myths, where she uses her sexuality to get hold of golden adornments, especially in *Sörla þáttr*, where she appears as Óðinn's mistress. One day she happened to see four dwarves working under a stone, forging a beautiful necklace. Freyja adored the necklace and the dwarves adored Freyja. When she began to bargain with them, they were unwilling to sell the adornment for any silver or gold in the world, but would give it to her if she would concede to sleep with them in turn the following nights. Freyja accepted, but Óðinn suspected her of adultery and stole the necklace with help of Loki. She had to confess her crime, but vowed to instigate a never-ending battle between two great kings in order to get her adornment back. This is the prelude to the story about the antagonists Heðinn and Högni and the battle between them, called Hjaðingavíg.[7]

Freyja's desire for gold coincides with the fact that she is surrounded by riches and even identified with the metal itself. She wears the famous *Brísingamen*, the adornment of Brísingr, as one of her attributes and her daughters are called Hnoss and Gersimi, meaning jewels. Her tears are said to be pure gold, a term often used in Skaldic *kenningar*.[8] *Grét ok at Óði gulli Freyja* "Freyja cried (tears of) gold for Óðr", as one example says.[9] Her gold and riches correspond with the two other Vanir's characteristics: Freyr is said to rule the prosperity of mankind[10] and Njörðr "is so rich and prosperous that he could give everyone abundance of land or personal propriety."[11] Freyr was the one who ruled agriculture and was evoked in the sacred formula *til*

---

7. The Sörla þáttr in Flateyjarbók, p. 391 ff., dating from the 11th century. The battle is mentioned already in Bragi's Ragnarsdrápa, about 800 AD and related in Snorri's Edda. Saxo's version reports that the battle took place on Hiddensee on Rügen and finally the folk-song Hildinakvedet from Shetland places the event on Orkney Island. Olav Bø, KLNM, s.v. Hjadingavíg.
8. Sksm. 30.
9. Snorra Edda, s. 199.
10. Glf. 23.
11. Loc.cit.

*árs ok fríðar* "for a (good) year's crop and peace", whereas Njörðr's domain was the sea and the riches from trade and fishing. The Vanir thus personified the good things of life, gold, fertility and voluptuousness.

Under the name of Menglöd, "fond of adornments", Freyja appears as a loving and yearning woman, who waited long for Svipdag's, i.e. Óðinn's, return to her bed in the poem called *Fjölsvinnsmál*. Even though this poem has been preserved as a Medieval romance, influenced by literary currents from the continent, some traits of the original theme of a *hieros gamos* between Óðinn and Freyja remain.

Freyja was often evoked as helper by women in childbirth and nursing. In the Eddic poem *Oddrúnargrátr* the exhausted mother after the delivery of twins blesses her helper with the words. "May the kind powers Frigg and Freyja help you as you have saved me from dangerous evil!" Several examples from folklore, like the belief in the helping function of the elder-tree (which was connected with Freyja),[12] or the formula after childbirth "Freyja may help you to feed and rock the child (to sleep)",[13] imply that she once carried this function, which later was transferred to the Virgin Mary.

Until now, we have presented Freyja solely as a fertility goddess. The great goddess of the North carries, however, other characteristics of equal prominence. She is a goddess of the highest rank, according to Snorri, "the most honourable besides Frigg".[14] Furthermore her name, Freyja, means 'the Lady' and is equivalent with the title 'fru' worn by wives of the nobility.

As we already mentioned, she appears as Óðinn's wife, although Snorri reserves this place for Frigg in his Edda. In this context he refers to a certain Óðr as Freyja's husband. He is always travelling far away and his absence causes the goddess to shed tears of pure gold. It is, however, not likely that Óðinn and

---

12. Reichborn-Kjennerud 1923: 22-23.
13. de Vries 1970 II: 311, n.1.
14. Glf. 36.

Óðr are two different mythological persons. Their names are both connected with the adjective óðr meaning 'furious', 'ecstatic', and alluding to Óðinn's special characteristics as the god of both magic and poetical inspirations and fury. Although the title Freyja is not derived from the same stem as Frigg, 'the beloved', the limits between them are indefinite. Originally of the same identity, they fulfil a similar religious function.[15]

Like Óðinn Freyja controls the skill of sorcery. She was the one who taught the Æsir seiðr, which was used by the Vanir, Snorri assumes.[16] Seiðr involved divination, but also all kinds of evil bewitchment and was an occupation for women only. The two sorceresses Gullveig and Heiðr, who appear in the war between the Æsir and the Vanir, were probably Freyja herself. According to Völuspá 21-22 they entered Hár's (Óðinn's) hall and attacked the gods with their witchcraft, distorting their minds and charming them by seiðr. Although the Æsir tried to pierce Gullveig with spears and burn her, she returned again.

When Loki addresses her with the words: "Be silent, Freyja, you are a sorceress, full of evil", he uses the word *fordæda*, 'evil-doer', a strong expression for a witch. We know from other examples, as Sörla þáttr, that she instigates the battle between Heðinn and Högni by using witchcraft. She distorts Heðinn's mind, which make him commit the most cruel deeds against Högni's family, forgetting his code of honour and sworn brotherhood.

Freyja's magical skill belongs to the same realm as her sacral characteristics. According to Snorri's strongly euhemerized account of the gods' arrival in the North, Óðinn, Njörðr and Freyr settled at Uppsala together with Freyja.[17] Here the gods became kings in turn and inaugurated the cult. In this connection it is explicitly told that Freyja acted as a blótsgyðja, 'a sacrificial

---

15. Näsström 1995: 104-111.
16. Hkr. 4.
17. Hkr. 4.

priestess' or 'a sacrificial goddess'.[18] She also became the one who, after the death of Óðinn, Njörðr and Freyr, maintained the sacrifices at Uppsala, Snorri recounts.

In the enumeration of the gods' heavenly abodes in Grímnismál, Freyja is said to live in Folkvangr, 'the Field of the Warriors', and she and Óðinn share the men slain on the battlefield. Snorri quotes this stanza and adds that "whenever she rides into battle she takes half of the slain". Freyja receives the slain heroes of the battlefield quite as respectfully as Óðinn does. Her house is called Sessrumnir, 'filled with many seats', and it probably fills the same function as Valhöll, 'the hall of the slain', where the warriors eat and drink beer after the fighting. Still, we must ask why there are two heroic paradises in the Old Norse View of afterlife. It might possibly be a consequence of different forms of initiation of the warriors, where one part seemed to have belonged to Óðinn and the other to Freyja.[19] These examples indicate that Freyja was also a war-goddess, and she even appears as a valkyrie, literally 'the one who chooses the slain'.[20]

As a receiver of the dead her abode is also open for women who have suffered a noble death. Thorgerðr, the daughter of Egil Skallagrímsson, makes a promise to starve herself to death, with the words "I will have no supper, and I don't want to have any before I am at Freyja's."[21] In the saga of Heiðrek the Wise the queen hangs herself in the dísarsalr 'the Hall of the Dís', when she discovers that her husband had betrayed her father and brother. This Dís could hardly be anyone but Freyja herself, the natural leader of the collective of female deities called dísir,[22] and the place of the queen's suicide seems thus to be connected with Freyja. The dominating idea among scholars that only warriors slain on the battle-field, "wounded by weapons",

---

18. Gyðja is the feminine form of goði 'priest', but could also mean 'goddess'.
19. About Freyja's role in initiation rites, see Näsström 1995: 151-175.
20. Näsström 1995: 86 ff.
21. Egils saga Skall-Grimsonar ch. 76.
22. Näsström 1995: 133.

were promised an afterlife, neglects the fact that the sources mention a place for women besides the gloomy dwellings of Hel.²³

Freyja thus carries many important qualities in addition to her identity as a goddess of love and fertility. These other qualities are, in most cases, neglected by historians of religions, since they do not fit in with the usual picture of the voluptuous Freyja, the Nordic counterpart of Aphrodite Pandemos.

More than anyone else, George Dumézil had examined the structure of the relation among different gods in the myths of the Indo-Europeans. But even he ignores the varying qualities of Freyja, since he took, in fact, very little interest in goddesses. Basically, he saw the goddesses of the North as split into two fractions, Frigg representing sovereignty in her position as Óðinn's wife, while the god of the third function, Freyr, left his name to Freyja, rich and pleasure-loving.²⁴ Since Frigg and Freyja originally were one and the same goddess, Dumézil's view does not help us any further in our analysis of the different qualities of Freyja.

However, he did venture a hypothesis considering the position of the goddess in the tripartite structure of the various Indo-Europeans pantheons. She is trivalent, carrying qualities corresponding to each of the three functions of the male gods, which means that she carries characteristics of the magico-religious, the warlike and the productive realm. These characteristics, according to Dumézil, belong to her Indo-European origin and are not, as usually suggested, expressions of syncretism.²⁵

In this respect each Indo-European goddess constitutes a

---

23. Ibid: 88; see also Roesdahl 1989: 72. A different suggestion was put forward by Sawyer 1992: 81. Sawyer suggests that the exclusion of women from Valhöll facilitated the Christian mission among the women. This conclusion might, in my opinion, be a misunderstanding in the same way that Western scholars earlier misinterpreted the Quran's description of paradise as a place where no women were allowed to enter.
24. Dumézil 1970: 300.
25. Loc.cit.

complement to the male triad, representing the magico-religious, the martial and the fertility aspects. Uniting these functions she serves as a counterbalance of the male gods, who each carry only one function, although she primarily occupies one function, usually the third.[26]

Dumézil illustrates his hypothesis with three great goddesses of Indo-European origin, the Iranians Anāhitā, the Vedic Sarasvatī and the Roman Juno. Anāhitā is in Yašt V, 85-87, evoked by the warriors, by her own priests and by the women.[27]

It is true that the text of this Yašt is corrupt, but still she is evoked with her entire name as Aredvī Sūrā Anāhitā 'the humid, the strong and the immaculate', elements reflecting the third, the second and the first function.[28]

A similar structure is found in the case of the Vedic Goddess Vāc, deified Speech, who presents herself as maintaining the male gods Mitra-Varuna (first function), Indra-Agni (the second) and the two Asvins (the third).[29] Vāc is no one else than the great goddess Sarasvatī; she is accompanied by the twin brothers, the two Asvins, and these three deities, caring for fertility in humans, beasts and soil, are the canonical representatives of the third function. It is said about Sarasvatī that she is the one who plants the embryo in the mother's womb.[30]

Nevertheless, Sarasvatī occupies other spheres of activity according to the Vedic hymns. Together with the two Āprī goddesses Idā or Ilā and Bhāratī, she is the means of purification connected with the animal sacrifice and she is also the one who accepts the sacrifice, thus representing the first function. But in other hymns she appears as a warlike figure, who attacks the enemies of the gods, and in this respect she carries the name Vṛtraghni, 'the destroyer of resistance', an epithet that she shares with Indra, the warrior god par preference.

---

26. Dumézil 1970: 298 f.
27. Loc.cit.
28. Lommel 1954: 405-413.
29. RV. 10.125.
30. RV. 10.184.2.

Dumézil's third example is the Roman Juno. In Lanuvium, a small city close to Rome, this goddess was worshipped as Juno S.M.R., short for Juno Seipithei Matri Reginae. Each of the epithets represents one of the three functions: Seipes (or Sospes or Sospita) is the warlike personage, Mater the producer and Regina the sovereignty. That Juno was a fertility goddess is well-known, especially in her aspect of Lucina, the helper at childbirth, and as Jupiter's wife she is the queen of heaven. Her role as warrior goddess, as Seipes or Martialis on coins, completes the triad of functions.[31]

Against this theory several voices had been raised in objection. Their principal criticism is based on the title regina, which was connected with Juno's (and Hera's) protection of cities and their connection with the kings, reges, who ruled the cities. Since cities belonged to a rather late phase of human society, it is argued that they could not possibly belong to the Indo-European concept. Some critics stated that Juno was a goddess for the women and for human fertility, and that was what developed her qualities as protector of the city.[32]

In my opinion this argument is not valid. The title regina might be connected with city-culture, but the goddess may have had a close connection with the leader of the society in an earlier stratum.[33] Moreover, it also alludes to her marriages with Jupiter and to the fact that she is highest in rank among the goddesses.

The title mater was, according to the criticism, in use for several goddesses and not specifically for Juno in her capacity of the third function. Juno has, however, a number of epithets which state her role in the third function like Pronuba and Jugalis, protectress of marriage or Fluonia (who stops menstruation when conception has taken place) and Lucina, the helper in childbirth.

---

31. Näsström 1995: 94.
32. Momigliano 1987: 135-159 and Simon 1990: 99.
33. Benveniste 1969 II: 4-5.

## Freyja – The Trivalent Goddess

There are, however, other problems with the cult of Juno in Lanuvium which Dumézil himself notes in his article 'Juno S.M.R.'. In this city a cult of Jupiter and Mars existed, but there is no sign of any worship of the third function, represented by Quirinus. It is also conspicuous that Juno does not carry the three functions in Rome, only the first, regina, and the third, Lucina, equivalent to mater.[34] Such deviations could be the result of historical development and no decisive argument against the theory of the Indo-European tripartite system. After all, the statues and the inscription 'Juno S.R.M.' do exist in Lanuvium.

In Ireland the 'Plain of Macha' played a certain role as the capital of the pagan kings. One story deals with three Machas, each with a different legend: one seer, one warlike princess, and one connected with fertility. Each of these Machas suffers a death related to her function in the tripartite scheme. The seer dies from a vision she had beheld, the warlike Macha is killed and the third dies in childbirth. These three women or deities carrying the name Macha are another example of the trivalence of the Indo-European goddess.[35]

We find other examples of this trivalent goddess when turning to the epics and folktales. In the Mahābhārata, Draupadī is said to be an incarnation of Śrī, the goddess of riches and fertility, who also holds tejas 'spiritual and magical power' and indriya 'physical power'.

Another example is found among the Caucasian Ossetes, whose folktales narrate about a princess called Sætanæ, whose qualities are definitely supernatural. The beautiful Sætanæ is an owner of gold, and according to one of the many legends she prevents a famine among her people. Yet she is described as strong, even aggressive and filled with magical power and might therefore be taken as an example of the trivalent goddess.

The myths of the trivalent goddess sometimes reveal a tension between male and female. There is the guileful goddess, like

---

34. Dumézil 1953: 115-119.
35. Dumézil 1954: 5-17.

Freyja in Sörla þáttr, who commits adultery, tempted by a gift of golden adornments. This figure might be regarded as an outlet of repressed feminine aspirations, reflected in both myths and rituals, but since we do not possess any extant sources concerning male-female tensions, we must consider other interpretations.[36]

The tension depends rather on conflicts and difficulties in co-operation not between the sexes but between social groups and kinship in society.[37] When conflicts appear in the myths they are changed into a model which tries to overcome them by repeating the motif over and over again, like the myths of the third function's struggle to become accepted by the first and the second. The contradiction was in reality impossible to surmount and therefore had to be repeated in order to express its message.[38] For this reason we may assume that conflicts between male and female deities in the Indo-European myths usually symbolise the conflict between the first two functions and the third in which case the goddesses represent the third.

A very conspicuous example is the Circe-episode in the Odyssey. Weather-driven Odysseus and his shipmates land on a foreign island. Half of his men go ashore to reconnoitre and to seek provisions when they come across the abode of the sorceress Circe. She appears as a friendly and beautiful woman who gives them a beverage to drink, but her intentions are black as night. The drink contains a potion that makes the men forget their home and origin and, what is more, they become transformed into pigs by Circe's magic wand. Crying, because they still possess the clear mind of a human being they are locked up in a pigpen, where death is their only hope of release.

---

36. The patriarchal structure of Indo-European marriage was expressed in terms of the man wedding the woman and the woman being wedded. No expression is found in the Indo-European language for the opposite condition, wherefore a marriage was a change of status for woman, not an action of her own intention. Benveniste 1969: 217 ff.
37. Lincoln 1981: passim.
38. Lévi-Strauss 1967: 226.

## Freyja – The Trivalent Goddess

One of the men, Elylochos, never drinks the potion and manages to escape before his shipmates are transformed into pigs. He tells Odysseus that they disappeared without any tracks. Odysseus decides to go ashore and see what happened to his men. Fortunately, the god Hermes appears and tells him about their fate. The god brings him an antidote and advises him how to handle Circe's sorcery. She welcomes him amiably as a new candidate for her pigpen and offers him a drink, but Hermes' antidote eliminates the magic potion. When she swings her wand Odysseus draws his sword and threatens her. As Hermes has foreseen, the sorceress now seeks to seduce him. Out of regard for his comrades, Odysseus does not resist, but asks her to swear an oath that she will not hurt him during the act of lovemaking.[39]

As Dumézil has suggested, the three methods employed by Odysseus correspond with the tripartite functions of the Indo-European society,[40] the herb belonging to the third function, the sword to the second and the oath to the first.[41]

As we shall see, the tripartite way to subdue a woman is a common element in Indo-European myths. At his first sight of the giantess Gerðr, Freyr falls in love and he immediately sends his servant Skírnir 'the shining one' to propose to the girl. Skírnir, who is a hypostasis of the god himself, finds Gerðr inimical to

---

39. This passage in the 10th book of the *Odyssey* has been compared with the story about Bedr basin and Queen Lab in *Arabian Nights*. The similarities between the passage in question are evident and it is definitively possible that some narrative elements in the *Odyssey* could appear in the *Arabian Nights*, influenced by Hellenistic novels. Such a narrative element about men, transfigured into animal by sorceress are well-know from Ovid's *Metamorphoses*. About the influences from the Hellenistic novels, see G.E. Grünebaum 1963.

    It has to be observed that the stories diverge more than they coincide. Odysseus was never changed into an animal like Bedr Basin and his men were. Furthermore Bedr Basin and Queen Lab exchange poison and antidotes and transform into various animals.
40. Dumézil 1982: 131.
41. Dumézil 1958: 21-22.

his errand. He begins to offer her golden apples and the ring Draupnir which produces eight golden rings every nine nights. Gerðr refuses icily. Skírnir threatens her with his sword, but she takes no notice. Then he utters a curse, loaded with maledictions, intensified when the poem changes its metre from ljóðaháttr into galdralag, the metre of spells:

> Listen giants, listen frost giants, sons of Suttungr, all kin of Æsir,
> How I deny, how I forbid the girl from man's joy, the girl from man's use!
> Hrímgrímnir is the giant, who shall have you down at the gates of Hel;
> where 'Vilmegir' will serve you goats' piss and you shall live on wooden roots.
> You will never get a nobler drink, of my will, of your will.
> I carve a þurs-rune for you and three staves: defilement, lechery and concupiscence!
> I will uncarve them like I (once) carved them, if that is needed.[42]

This curse breaks Gerðr's resistance and she makes Skírnir a promise to meet Freyr in the grove of Barri.

It is evident that the three different methods that Skírnir uses to subdue Gerðr are parallels to those which Odysseus used against Circe: first, gold and riches, like herbs, represent the third function; then follows the sword, representing the second, and finally the force of the words, a spell or an oath, as typical of the first function.

A third example supports our hypothesis that this pattern is inherent in Indo-European myths: Saxo Grammaticus' chronicle *Gesta Danorum* narrates how Óðinn (Othinus), seeking revenge for the killing of his son Baldr (Balderus), is told that he must beget a son with the princess Rinda.

---

42. Skírnismál 34-36. My translation.

## Freyja – The Trivalent Goddess

Óðinn's tactics now follow the pattern we have already seen in the examples of Odysseus and Skírnir. He tries to overcome her resistance with gold and riches, but the girl refuses. Then he has to change his role and become a fighter.[43] His military actions, representing the second function, are unsuccessful, and by cutting runes on a piece of bark he turns Rinda mad. This represents his magic skills and thereby the first function, the magico-religious. To complete the pattern, Óðinn appears as a sorceress, when fulfilling his evil intent. We know from other sources that he feels no shame to disguise as a woman.[44] His magical talent is underscored by the name Vecha (> witch), under which he enters the sick maiden's chamber and eventually manages to rape her and beget his son.

This repeated pattern shows a situation in which a god or a hero subdues a goddess for sexual intercourse, which might reflect a *hieros gamos*. It is obvious that the god/hero has to appeal to each of the three functions in a specific order, from the third to the first. When the first function appears in the form of the magic word, she opens her arms for her lover. It is true that Rinda in Saxo's version suffers a brutal rape. This may, however, be due to the general tendency of the Christian author to describe the licentious and ruthless nature of the pagan gods. Even the mild-mannered Baldr becomes a genuine brute in Saxo's version.

The fact that both Gerðr and Rinda belonged to the giants and not the goddesses, might seem to contradict the idea of the trivalent goddess subdued by triple means. It is, however, important to remember that the only myths extant are those in which the *hieros gamos* aspect has been transferred to the giantesses, as Gro Steinsland has shown in her thesis *Det hellige bryllop og Norrøn kongeideologi*.[45]

---

43. It is true that Óðinn appears at the court the first time as a warrior. This episode, however, obviously belongs to the passage of the mead of poetry.
44. Ls. 24.
45. Steinsland 1989: passim.

Odysseus versus Circe, Freyr-Skírnir versus Gerðr and Óðinn versus Rinda: in all these cases the woman is subdued by elements of the three functions of Indo-European myth. This expresses the idea that the trivalent goddess must be encountered by the three functions, when her male partner tries to coerce or inveigle her into a *hieros gamos*. The recurrent pattern of their attempts begins, as we have seen, with the third function and ends with an oath, a curse or a spell, i.e. the first function.

The implicit meaning of these myths is, however, as we already stated, that the first function is superior to the other two. The victorious magical word represents the sovereign, able to subdue the most reluctant goddess.

We have tried to prove that these examples of the trivalent Indo-European goddess show that we are dealing with a pattern corresponding to the triad of male gods ruling the tripartite functions, according to Dumézil's theory. Still, one important objection remains: is the trivalent goddess found anywhere else in the history of religions? The most important goddess of ancient Mesopotamia was the Sumerian Inanna, called Ishtar in Akkadian. Her name means 'Queen of Heaven', and she is sometimes the daughter of the moon god Nanna, sometimes of Enlil, the god of the atmosphere, or even of Enki, the earth god. Inanna's personality is divided between her aspects of love and of war. Inanna's love of Dumuzi is the mythical example of the sacred marriage rite in which the king of the Sumerian city symbolically weds the goddess, who is represented by her priestess.[46] In this respect, Inanna represents the cosmic force of fertility and abundance, and kings compete for her favour in terms of jealous lovers, boasting of their success in her bed.[47]

Her warlike aspect is in the same way connected with the king. She stays beside him in the battle, 'the playground of Ishtar', and she helps him to extend his power. The stories about her campaign against Mount Ebih, as well as her descent to the

---

46. Jacobsen 1970: 27-29.
47. Hallo and van Dink 1968: 6-10.

underworld, are expressions of her unlimited desire to expand her sphere of power.[48]

A third aspect of Inanna is her appearance as the planet Venus, 'Inanna of the sunrise'.[49]

It is true that this goddess has certain similarities whith the Nordic Freyja, being a goddess of love and sexual desire and a warrior goddess at the same time. Still, these characteristics are universally applicable to many goddesses from different cultures. The differences between Inanna and the Indo-European goddesses are more distinct: She has no male spouse permanently connected to her. Even her relationship with Dumuzi is rather ambiguous, whereas Freyja, Juno and the other mentioned goddesses are usually linked with at least one male partner, sometimes three, each of them representing one of the functions of the tripartite system.

Inanna's desire for love corresponds with her desire for land and in this respect she is the ideal goddess for any power-seeking king in the old Sumerian society. He consorts with her in a sacred marriage, and she is said to stand by his side in the battle.

We do not find any of these traits in myths about the Indo-European goddesses. They are, as we already mentioned, not exclusively connected with the kings but with the three different classes of society, priest-kings, warriors and producers.

Returning to Freyja, I believe to have established that she belongs to the traditional Indo-European pattern of the trivalent goddess and is much more than merely a fertility and a love goddess. Freyja's different functions of love and war, of magic and sovereignty thus correspond with those of the great goddesses of the Vedic, Iranian and Roman Pantheon. They form an example of the trivalent goddess who is a counterpart of each of the three male gods in the Indo-European tripartite system. The image of Freyja as merely 'rich and pleasure-loving' has to be revised in this comparative perspective.

---

48. Jacobsen 1976: 137-138.
49. Ibid.: 138-139.

# Bibliography

**Sources**
Apuleius. *The Golden Ass. Being the metamorphose of Lucius Apuleius*. Trans. W. Adlington, rev. S. Gaseler. 1927. London.
Eddadikte: *Gudadikte*, ed Jón Helgason. 1964. Oslo
Glf. = "Gylfaginning", see *Snorri Sturlasson Edda*.
Hdl.= "Hyndluljóð" see Eddadikte: *Gudadikte*
Hkr.= *Heimskringla* I, ed. Bjarni Aðalbjarnarson.1951. Reykjavík.
*Ovid's Metamorphoses* I-II. Trans. F.S. Miller. 1919. London.
*Ragnarsdrápa*, see *Snorri Sturlasson Edda*.
RV. = *Der Rig-Veda*. Trans. K.F. Geldner.1951. Wiesbaden.
*Saxonia Gesta Danorum*, ed. J. Olrik and H. Raeder. 1931. København.
Skm= "Skirnismál" se Eddadikte: *Gudadikte*.
*Snorri Sturlason Edda*, ed. Finnur Jónsson. 1926. København.
*The Saga of king Heidrek the Wise*, ed. C. Tolkien. 1960. London.

**Secondary literature**
Benveniste, É. 1969. *Le vocabulaire des institutions indoeuropéennes* I-II. Paris.
Bø, O. s.v. "Hjadingavíg", *KLNM*.
Dumézil, G. 1953. "Juno S.R.M." *Eranos* LI: 105-119.
–. 1954. "The trio des Macha." *Revue de l'histoire des religions* 146: 5-17.
–. 1958. *L'ideologie tripartie des Indo-Européens*. Bruxelles.
–. 1970. *Roman Archaic Religion*. Chicago.
–. 1981. *Apollon sonore et autre essais*. Paris.
Gnoli, G. 1990. "Anāhitā." In M. Eliade, ed., *Encyclopedia of Religions*. Chicago.
Grünebaum, G. E. 1963. *Der Islam im Mittelalter*. Chicago.
Hallo, W. and van Dink, J.J. 1963. *The Exaltion of Inanna*. New Haven and Yale.
Holtsmark, A. s.v. "Vali", *KLNM*.
Jacobsen, T. 1970. *Towards the Image of Tammuz and other Essays*. Cambridge, Mass.
–. 1976. *The Treasures of Darkness*. New Haven and London.
KLNM = *Kulturhistorisk lexikon för nordisk medeltid*. 1982. Malmö.
Lévi-Strauss, C. 1967. *Structural Anthropology*. New York.
Lincoln, B. 1981. *Priest, Warriors and Cattle*. Berkeley.
Lommel, H. 1954. "Anāhitā-Sarasvatī." In *Festschrift Friedrich Weller*. Leipzig.
Momigliano, A. 1987. *Ottavo contributo alla storia degli studi classici e del mondo antico*. Roma.
Näsström, B-M. 1992. "The Goddesses of Gylfaginning." In Ulfar Bragason, ed., *Snorrastefna*. Reykjavík.
–. 1995. *Freyja – the Great Goddess of the North*. Lund.
Reichborn-Kjennerud, I. 1927. "Vår gamle trolldomsmedicin." In *Skrifter utgitt av det Norske Videnskabsakademi*. Oslo.

Roesdahl, E. 1989. *Vikingernes verden.* København.
Sawyer, B. 1992. *Kvinnor och familj i det forn- och medeltida Skandinavien.* Skara.
Schjødt, J.P. 1991. "Relationerna mellan aser och vaner och dess ideologiske implikationer." In G. Steinsland et alia, eds., *Nordisk hedendom: et symposium.* Odense.
Simon, E. 1990. *Die Götter der Römer.* München.
Steinsland, G. 1991. *Det hellige bryllop og norrøn kongeideologi.* Larvik.
Ström, F. 1961. *Nordisk hedendom.* Göteborg.
Turville-Petre, G. 1964. *Myth and Religion of the North.* London.
de Vries, J. 1970. *Altgermanische Religionsgeschichte* I-II. Berlin.

# Verbal Representation of Religious Beliefs: A Dilemma in the Phenomenology of Religions

*Tord Olsson*
UNIVERSITY OF LUND, SWEDEN

The various attributes which the Maasai ascribe to God in their oral literature, and the idioms and rituals in which they figuratively express their relation to him in speech and action, are all in some way modes of phrasing or representing their religious notions, their "belief" or "faith". However, I soon realized during my field-work that it would be a mistake to consider such processes as simple externalizations of mental attitudes. The Maasai do not simply "believe" in everything they actually say, although what they say may, nevertheless to themselves, be adequate expressions of what they believe. And if they "believe", there may be various degrees and modes in which they believe.

Neither can we observe any direct correspondance in the other direction which would allow us to regard "belief" and "faith" as simple internalizations of traditionally patterned formulas and rites. What concerns me here is not the psychological aspects of this problem, but the semantic. We will frequently find that a concrete and simple, sometimes even a paradoxical, expression stands for a coherent set of ideas which is not possible to grasp from the literal meaning of the expression. On the other hand, a singular and relatively simple notion may be expressed figuratively in a number of ways.

In particular, certain passages of prayers and some basic mythic elements furnish notorious problems of interpretation that are not, in the first instance, of linguistic nature or the result of idiomatic language usage. We are often in a position to produce a linguistically accurate translation or to explain an idiom without any understanding of its "inner" meaning and without any knowledge of what "belief" it may possibly indicate. Compared to the philologically oriented historian of religions, however, the fieldworker is in a privileged position: he can ask his informants.

Based on the indigenous exegesis thus acquired, we may eventually succeed in producing a reasonable interpretation of a linguistic expression or a textual element and obtain some idea of the "belief" involved. In practice, I have found this type of procedure illuminating. Indigenous exegesis provides an indispensable source for the study of religion and personal religiosity and has, as such, a value in its own right, irrespective of its relation to the text commented upon, and despite obvious problems of validity and reliability. Such exegesis is, as a rule, personally coloured, gives way to individual opinion, and is often as figuratively formulated as the topic commented upon, using metaphors to explain metaphors and so forth.

At some stage of the interpretative proceeding, it may appear that indigenous exegesis deviates from or extends beyond what has been stated in the oral text being commented upon. Hence, it can not be employed as an unproblematic device for interpretation, which demonstrates that there is a far from simple correspondence between "belief" and verbal realization, especially as far as religious literature is concerned. If, however, it is at all possible to demonstrate which "belief" is connected with or expressed by a given textual element or ritual, the indigenous interpretation of it should be considered as a source of primary range. After all, it is chiefly through what is said in the traditional texts themselves, and through language in the main, that we can hope to understand with precision anything at all about Maasai attitudes towards God.

In view of these considerations, indigenous exegesis may appear as a far more important source for "belief" than the texts themselves. Nevertheless, it is textual elements from prayer and myth, and ritual action and symbolism, that furnish the foundation for belief. This observation is not based on the condition of my query leading to such exegesis, but on the fact that the Maasai themselves constantly rely on traditional elements of religious literature and ritual for evidence in support of a "belief" or in arguing in favour of a given religious opinion.

If, from my discussions with the Maasai, I have rightly understood this elusive problem, it is not only that a textual or ritual element is considered as a contractive expression of a "belief" or a complex of ideas; they also tend to regard "beliefs" as mental modes or attitudes resulting from participation in ritual and from the performance of traditional literature. We may recall a gloss to Wittgenstein that Mayo has elaborated: "Having a belief is not having something which favourably disposes me towards something else – the fact believed – but rather, to have a belief is to be favourably disposed towards something else: to asserting (or accepting) the proposition believed".[1] To the Maasai, moreover, such favourable disposition towards asserting or accepting propositions expressed in prayer or myth results from participation in the performance of this literature itself. "Belief" is not only a motivation for performing a prayer or a rite; the latter are also considered as motives for holding "beliefs".

Besides "belief" as a mere intellectual assent, such as "belief" in the existence of God which Maasai consider as *e-yiolounoto* 'knowledge' or 'recognition', the dimension of "faith" or "trust" appears to involve traditional ways of action. This attitude implies a distinctive way of discussing religious matters and providing evidence for the embrace of certain "notions", "beliefs", "faiths", "norms", "values" etc. If possible, a Maasai will thus prefer to argue by means of adducing empirical examples from traditional oral and ritual behavior rather than referring to states of mind or offering theoretical reasons. For example, a person may hold that God either *is* the sky or is *in* the sky, or he may be indifferent or flexible regarding these propositions. In any of these cases he may support his opinion with reference to religious behavior: that people look upwards when they pray,

---

1. Mayo 1967: 161; Needham 1972: 60.

sprinkle milk towards the sky when they sacrifice etc. If he holds one of the two former opinions, but after discussion admits that the argument proves only that God is above *(shumata, keper)* he will most likely, in this case, dismiss the problem by saying e.g. "I personally do not know" *(mayiolo nanu)* or that it is "God alone who knows" *(enkAi nayiolo openy)*. If he is profoundly concerned, he may provide new evidence, but again with reference to traditional oral texts or ritual rather than theoretical arguments. Indeed, a rather critical attitude towards certain oral traditions can be observed, and is reflected, in recurrent phrases like "it is said that," "but others say," "personally I do not know, but some say." Moreover, this attitude is related to the important, but complicated ideals of wisdom *(engeno)* and respect *(enkanyit)*, which imply not only extensive knowledge and elaborate use of traditions, but also a capacity to listen and evaluate what people say. To a great extent, a man's authority rests on these abilities, by which he attracts people "like a tree and its shadow attract people without forcing them". In this sense a wise and respected man is said to have *oloip*, 'shadow'. Now, if a myth-teller wishes to persuade his audience that a certain variant is more reliable than others, he will not simply state that this is the case. Indeed, he may not even produce arguments to support his opinion. Rather, he will mention all the variants, but perform his favorite version in a way convincing to the listeners.

In mythical discourse, the relation between God and primeval man is described in rather concrete terms. God was close to man in a spatial sense, abiding on earth and, originally, at the same place *(ewueji)* as man. God used to speak to man and give him things for his subsistence. But then it happened that God 'settled' *(netonie)* in his own place, that is, his own kraal camp, his own place, where he settled by himself *(ewueji enye, duo enkang enye, ewueji enye natonie openy)*, and eventually 'God cursed man' *(nedek apa ankAi oltungani)* and ascended *(neilep)* to heaven.[2] Mythical description, then, represents God and his interaction

---

2. Cf. Olsson 1975-82, II: 22-52.

with man in concrete and rather anthropomorphic terms. Now, if such passages of myth were considered literally true, they would, of course, provide evidence concerning the nature of God. In view of indigenous interpretation of myth, however, this is not consistent with Maasai ways of thinking. On the contrary, the Maasai generally insist that myth *(enkiterunoto)* is a particular literary genre with a language usage of its own, following certain stylistic rules, that it shall be performed in a special way and in a certain type of speech situation (after dark) with certain standardized questions posed by the audience etc.

According to Maasai exegesis, the anthropomorphic representation of the Divinity in myth is a characteristic of dramatic discourse itself and of the genre as such; but theologically speaking, this does not imply that God himself is equipped with anthropomorphic features. In this respect, myth is not considered "true" in a literal sense. What the Maasai conclude from myth is that primeval man somehow had a direct experience of God and from this knew his nature, but what this experience really meant is not known any more. Therefore, 'concerning God, there is no human being who can know what God used to be like' *(ore enkAi metii hoo tungani oidim atayiolo ajo kaji apa eikununo enkAi)*.

In the oral literature of the Maasai the hymns to *enkAi* 'God' constitute the most concentrated form of religious verbal expression. Within oral tradition they form a distinct genre called *osinkolio le nkAi*, "song to God". Since the texts are dominated on the one hand by their specific hymnal character, but also by prayer to *enkAi*, which at times assumes a familiar or even ironic tone, they perhaps more than other genres express a characteristic representation of god determined by the tension between *a feature of nature* and the *personal or anthropomorphic* configuration. On the level of expression, God is identified primarily with the visible heaven, but also with heavenly bodies, the earth and other elements of nature. On the other hand, the Maasai simultaneously implore a personal god and do so in rather anthropomorphic terms. I give one example here, a hymn sung by Melua enole Kamilo and other women in a kraal camp called Olokila, Loita, Kenya (recorded on 19.8 1974):

1. *asai naitorit ai enkolong*
2. *maek ai enteentei*
3. *atasaia ildapashi ooiririori*
4. *maek ai enteentei*
5. *asai ole nkai aidipa enkop*
6. *maek ai enteentei*
7. *enteentei ai milo iloreren*
8. *maek ai enteentei*
9. *milo Purko nimilo Kisonko*
10. *maek ai enteentei*
11. *nimiruk alo Oldoinyo le Sanya*
12. *maek ai enteentei*
13. *tobiko maikuso te Seiyai*
14. *maek ai enteentei*
15. *intoyie Oldionyo Loltarakua*
16. *maek ai enteentei*
17. *ayeleyio*
18. *ehoo alikiaomon ai enkai o enkop*
19. *enkayioni ntoyie selenkei*
20. *ayeleyio*
21. *maek ai enteentei*
22. *enkAi irrugu nkonyek abori ai*
23. *maek ai enteentei*

Translation:
1. You pray to the one which is centred by the sun
2. you who do not give me trouble
3. I have prayed to the wide parallel ones
4. you who do not give me trouble
5. (and) I pray to that of the sky after (praying to) the earth
6. you who do not give me trouble
7. you who do not give me trouble, do not go to (other) tribes
8. you who do not give me trouble
9. don't go to Purko and don't go to Kisonko
10. you who do not give me trouble
11. and don't agree to go to Oldoinyo le Sanya
12. you who do not give me trouble

13. stay and dwell at Seiyai
14. you who do not give me trouble
15. (so say) the girls from Oldoinyo Loltarakua
16. you who do not give me trouble
17. *ayeleyio*
18. *ehoo* O you to whom we pray, sky and earth
19. (for) a little boy, girls, a little girl
20. *ayeleyio*
21. you who do not give me trouble
22. God, turn your eyes down to me
23. you who do not give me trouble[3]

Historians of religion have considered such contrasting representations of God as the result of a development from nature divinity to a personal divinity, or, the other way around. However, it should be noted that the Maasai themselves do not generally conceive of this tension as an opposition on the cognitive level.

To whom or to what, then, did the women from Olokila turn when they sang this hymn to *enkAi*? The words in the prayer were directed to the wide-stretched sky, centred by the sun, and to the earth as seen within the eyes' span; but at the same time to the one *in* the sky (or *"of"* the sky, *ole nkai*, line 5), to the one who should remain with Loita's women and make them fruitful, not fleeing to other tribes; to God who should turn his eyes upon the prayerful, and not cause distress.

I asked Melua enole Kamilo, who answered: "The earth is god *(ore enkop enkai)*. They (sky and earth) are the same god, one god *(enkai nabo)*, since we worship them in the same fashion. God *(enkAi)* is above *(shumata)* and below *(abori)*. He is everywhere *(pooki wueji).*" Another woman concurred: "We pray to the earth *(enkop)* first, and then to the sky *(enkai)*, but they are the same god, one god *(enkai nabo).*" I inquired as to what was meant by the expression "your eyes". She answered: "We don't know whether God has eyes or not, because nobody has seen

---

3. Olsson 1975-82, I: 23-32.

him. Maybe he has, because he can see everything. He can kill anybody he wants because of that."

It is not beyond the realm of possibilities that through their poetic form the hymns have preserved archaic features – linguistically, some formulations would indicate this – and therefore, to a greater extent than other literary types, they reflect more ancient conceptualizations of God. However, to show this through historical methods would prove difficult because of the poor quality of the few available early writings. Therefore, the question of which conceptualization comprises the "original" cannot be determined from existing documents; perhaps God as identical with the firmament, or God as a personal being who dwells in heaven. On the other hand, it is far from self-evident that there exists any *chronological relation* at all between the personal and the natural features in the representation of Divinity. From Maasai oral texts and from what Maasai say themselves, I would rather conclude that these features appear as *simultaneous dimensions*, even in one and the same text or in the same utterance stated by an individual person, and there is no evidence to prove that this is the result of any recent development.

Besides, there is an observable distribution of these features with respect to literary form, genre, or speech situation. The natural features are thus lacking in the mythical discourse, but found in the typical hymnic passages of *isinkolioitin le nkAi*, whilst the personal or anthropomorphic features are expressed in the petitional passages of the hymns and in the frame of mythic narrative.

The various representations of Divinity are thus conditioned by literary genre and speech situation. Instead of dealing with this problem in historical terms, we can treat it synchronically as a literary and sociolinguistic one and, within this frame, investigate its semantic and cognitive aspects.

To sum up, it would be misleading to say that one or another natural element or anthropomorphic category dominates Maasai representation of God as a whole or has ever done so. Rather, the situation is that different understandings dominate in different speech contexts; and with reference to oral literature, given conceptions find expression in given genres. Thus, some religious beliefs are formulated most readily in the poetic form of hymns: primary examples include expressions of God's majesty in his diverse manifestations, such as the identification of the divine with the firmament, earth and other natural elements. In the petitionary passages of hymns and in recited prayer, *enkomono*, we find, on the other hand, concrete imagery in which features such as pain and anger are given literary expression as human qualities.

This dimension of the divine is, otherwise, expressed foremost in mythical discourse: here, God appears in anthropomorphic form as an individual person who originally lived on earth, who converses with people and intermingles with the other *dramatis personae* of the myth. When religious texts become the objects of interpretation in an exegetical or theological speech situation, it is important to emphasize the text's specific literary character and to note that the appropriate expression of divinity takes the form of simile and metaphor. The text's figurative expression is, thus, often further explained by imagery and analogy. Theologically however, exegesis is dominated by an aspiration towards balance, synthesis and intellectualization of the obvious tension and concretion of the image of God which converge in a given text. (Because of my presence, the analysis was philologically and ethnographically explanatory as well).

Myth is an orally transmitted narrative account. There is reason to assume that it achieves status as a tradition largely because it is considered a good narrative and bearer of a vital message. Its survival through the process of cultural selection (in competition with other narratives) depends on its literary qualities, mnemotechnical peculiarities, impressive formulation characteristics and its dramatic structure. The myth in its entirety is not, however, normally understood by the Maasai as a "true" narrative in the sense of an exact description of a factual primeval event; but, it is nevertheless an *adequate* description, relevant for the universe and life in the transmitter's environment.

A fundamentalistic acceptance of and unreflected belief in

myth is ridiculed and considered naive and credulous. If, indeed, a mythic episode is depicted as "true" or declared an object of "belief" by the transmitters of tradition, attention must then be given to the criteria of truth upon which the claims are based, and what, in the special case, is meant by "truth" and "belief". Most often we find pragmatic truth criteria, by which the *outcome* of what is conveyed in the myth is in agreement with factual conditions, morality, rules and values. According to Maasai cosmogony, God sent down cattle by a rope *(enkeene)* from heaven to the first man on earth who was a Maasai. This is why the Maasai people are now cattle owners. In declaring a mythical episode "true," reference is usually made to prevailing conditions. What is meant is that the episode is an adequate account of present circumstances, but seldom that the myth is literally true. That given aspects of a myth are considered true – if even a comparable term were used – results from an interpretation of the mythic text, with a greater or lesser amount of abstraction and structuring of the narrative text. This occurs most often in connection with narration and occasionally during the narration situation itself. During this particular hermeneutic procedure, the narrator emphasized both for the audience and especially for me as an outsider that myth narration was one means of transmitting traditional knowledge, and that this had been learnt from former generations. It was also pointed out that transmission included the narrative's content as well as its literary form (for example a special introductory formulation), plus the narrative technique itself with questions and answers from the audience. In addition, the narration act by tradition must be held after dark, following the day's work to allow for greater participation.

Thus, myth consists of traditional knowledge transmitted in a special manner, and to which belongs the narrative's dramatic structure determined by antagonism and associational relationships between the mythic actors. A good story-teller knows how to exploit this in a skilled fashion, whereas, in a hermeneutic conversational situation, it is of little or no importance. Indeed, at times it is denied that certain dramatic elements are true;

they simply comprise the form into which traditional knowledge is stuffed. They belong to the narrative's literary components, which are essential for the course of events and drama, but are not always objects of belief. This may be intimated in narrative techniques of voice and gesture, and by the attitude of the teller and the audience. When myth is interpreted in hermeneutic conversational situations, one approaches a view that in practice implies that the *cosmogony* is interpreted as a symbolic *cosmology* here coded in narrative form. It is the cosmological system rather than the narrative elements that is conceived of as "true" or as objects of "belief".

It should be pointed out that the attitude of the Maasai concerning myths diverges somewhat from the typologies of narrative texts developed by anthropologists, folklorists and historians of religion, who assume that certain genres, including myths, are considered true in their entirety while other narratives simply exercise an entertaining function. For the Maasai, the borderline for "truth" and "belief" runs through the mythic genre itself, being altered according to the situation and narrator; certain components are considered "true" and are objects of "belief", others are not. In mythical texts, *enkAi* is characterized in anthropomorphic terms. He dwells, at first, in the same camp (*enkang*) as primeval man, he owns cattle, converses and mingles with human beings, is frightened of being struck by women and ascends to heaven via the rope (all mimically illustrated by the narrator who, with vocal alterations, acts out all the roles including the god's). This is, however, seldom understood in exegetical conversations as literally true. According to the transmitters themselves, the story signifies that God and humans stood in a closer relationship primevally than they do at present. In this respect, the manifest characterization of God within the framework of mythic discourse does not lend expression to a common conception of God among the Maasai.

Myth constitutes a narrative account of a more or less dramatic primeval event involving the gods. Usually the gods assume a central position as narrative components in the complex of positive and antagonistic relations of mythic discourse, and their characterization is positionally determined by the way they interact with other *dramatis personae* in the narrative. This interaction is usually expressed in terms of individual human relations: antagonism, power relations, acts of violence, obedience and disobedience, dialogue, erotic and emotional relations etc.

The narrative genre's internal demands for clarity and drama also tend to produce the effect that the gods are depicted visually in concrete personal categories and appear in anthropomorphic forms. The anthropomorphic representation of God can often be seen as a formal characteristic of the mythic genre that does not automatically imply corresponding "beliefs."

In Maasai religion, traditional literature is still transmitted orally without a written medium. The obvious advantages of this from a research point of view include that the performance can be observed directly and that the representation of God within the framework of the oral text can be confronted with the transmitter's own interpretation in exegetical and theological dialogue situations. Through the comparison of textual and metatextual statements, it is possible to determine which elements of the representation derive from conventions of the literary genre and which are expressions of a generally comprised conception of God.

As a primary result of these observations, we can establish that anthropomorphism in the representation of God, as well as other components of myth, certainly comprise *theologumena* within the framework of the mythical narrative and in the petitionary passages of prayers; however, this should not be thought of as pronouncements of a commonly comprised *theologia*.

When we have no access to oral information from the transmitters of tradition, the problem of interpretation is much more difficult. The emic meaning of a document is especially difficult to find out.

When dealing with religions of the past we may instead use documentation like commentaries – which can be very comprehensive – or glosses inserted into texts, which are especially common in translation literature, such as Pahlavi texts. But apart from this restriction to written media – and the communicational shortcomings involved with it – in principle the procedure is the same.

In the field of Old Egyptian religion, the Heidelberg egyptologist Jan Assmann has recently presented ideas on the same line as the more experimental enquiries I have instituted among the Maasai. But of course he has set out from a different basis. What concerns me now, is that Assman's investigation is carried out in a religion where the so called "concept of god" has consistently been described as "*anthropomorphic*" or "*theriomorphic*". In earlier research these terms have also been used to represent stages of development in the history of Egyptian religion;[4] just as among the Maasai, the nature aspect and the personal aspect of God have been assumed to represent stages in a historic development. However, in Egypt we have a multitude of gods, and they appear on different levels, or in different dimensions of religious reality: (1) the cosmic; (2) the cultic; and (3) the mythic.

Let us look at the mythic dimension: The representation ('A') of a certain god (A) is conditioned by the social stratification in the society of gods, and by the position of this particular god (A) within this structure. This is expressed in terms of power and kinship, by means of which the particular god (A) is related to other gods. The representation of the god is also expressed by divine actions, which take place within the constellation of certain roles. On the mythical level the gods are thus interactionally connected with each other within a pattern of given roles. Some examples:

> Horus: "His father's avenger (*nḏ-ḥr-jtj.f*)
> Anubis: "Embalmer'
> Thot: "Secretary", "writer", "Minister" etc.
> Geb: "Judge"

In mythic discourse the gods appear in their "biotic" sphere – they eat and drink, they love and hate, they suffer and act in a human way. Now, these narratives should not be misunderstood

---

4. E.g. Morenz 1960: 20.

as theological statements. They are *theologoumena*, but not part of a *theologia*. This "biotics" is not part of the essence of the divine; rather it is a necessary part of the nature of narrative. Only in this sense is it a basic structural element in the mythic dimension.[5] Just as in the example from the Maasai, the anthropomorphic representation of god is conditioned by the formal characteristics of the literary genre of "myth". Again, we can not automatically conclude that the representations of the gods in "myth" are immediate expressions of religious beliefs, in the sense of what the old Egyptians figured to be the real essence of the gods. Contrasting with mythic narrative, there are in fact texts that relate divine epiphany, in which a divinity reveals itself to individual persons, in its "divine shape or form" (*jrw n ntr*). The representations of divinities in such accounts, however, appear as curiously hazy and vague.

Let us have a look at such a "revelation text". When the god Amun approached the slumbering queen Iahmes in order to beget the succeeding queen Hatshepsut, "the palace abounded with divine fragrance". The queen is awakened by the smell, which is the first sign of divine presence, before the divinity reveals itself in its true "divine shape", and before it takes form in the shape of Thutmosis.[6]

In texts of this type the account is quite brief and scantily worded, restrained and moderate – it is about feelings, vague indications, and the influence produced by the divinity – but certain recurring motifs can be seen: the "fragrance" (*stj* = lit. "the outflow, streaming forth"), for instance, by means of which the gods intimate (rather than announce) their presence. There is so much evidence of this kind of terminology referring to gods that we can speak of a fairly standardized way of expression. When Hatshepsut herself is described according to this pattern – the fragrance of her body and her shining skin are mentioned

---

5. Assmann 1977: 769 f.
6. *Urk.* IV: 220,5 = 1714,16 and 220,1 = 1714,12; Brunner 1964: 35-38 with plate 4; Hornung 1973: 122 f.

– it is her "divine essence" (*nṯrj* = lit. "god-being, being divine") that is emphasized.[7]

By contrasting different types of texts in this way, I have tried to illuminate conditions that appear paradoxical: In a religion like the Egyptian, where the *representation of god* in myth and iconography is illustrated in so graphic or plastic a way, we meet a number of texts in which "the form" of the divine is described in very vague and intimating terms. If the collocation "divine form" is an expression for what the old Egyptians considered to be the real nature of the gods, this would possibly be the most immediate expression of their *notion of the divine* that we can find. Consequently the rich iconography and the abundant mythic texts that are so typical of Egyptian religion, should not be mistaken as any direct expressions of theology or any doctrinal statements about the true nature of gods.

A similar contrast evident in Greek religion received considerable attention, not least by scholars at Lund University, like Martin Nilsson and Erland Ehnmark.[8] The course of events in the Homeric epics follows two parallel lines: The action takes place partly on the stage of the gods, partly on the stage of human beings. The events in the human world are caused by the gods, often by direct intervention. Scholars have long since observed that such events are described in two different fashions: first, as experienced by the human actors, in which case direct speech is placed in their mouths. Second, the course of events is also described from the "Olympian perspective". Now, the passages written in direct speech are remarkably vaguely formulated: It is said, for instance, that "a god" (*tis theos*), "the gods", or "one of the gods" are involved, but no closer explanations are given.

In contrast, within the Olympian perspective, the gods assume human shape. They are named, their appearance, character, and internal relations are described in concrete terms. – So,

---

7. *Urk.* IV: 339 f.; 15 f.; Hornung 1973: 123 f.
8. Nilsson 1964: 162 ff.; Ehnmark 1939: 29.

with minor changes, a model like the one I outlined for describing Egyptian mythology could be applied here as well.

Opinions differ about the religious significance of these two narrative perspectives. I shall not go into details here – suffice it to say that there are, once more, development theories: The phenomenon is interpreted according to same general model of historical development, or, according to some theory of psychological priorities. – However, such interpretations can not be confirmed by means of internal criteria in the Homeric texts or other literary documents of later date. Rather, such interpretations have an *ad hoc* character and are strongly dependent on general theories.

For my purpose, such episodes where the same event is described from two different narrative perspectives are particularly interesting. Consider one example where the text conveys a double exposure of one and the same event.

> ... and before them Pallas Athene, bearing a golden lamp, made a most beauteous light. (35) Then Telemachus suddenly spoke to his father, and said:
> "Father, verily this is a great marvel that my eyes behold; certainly the walls of the house and the fair beams and cross-beams of fir and tile pillars that reach on high, glow in my eyes as with the light of blazing fire. (40) Surely some god is within, one of those who hold broad heaven."
> Then Odysseus of many wiles answered him, and said: "Hush, check thy thought, and ask no question; this, I tell thee, is the way of the gods that hold Olympus ..."[9]

The situation is this: Ulysses has returned home. Only Telemachus has recognized him. They are planning the assassination of the suitors – and the goddess Pallas Athena gives them a hand. They have to hide away their weapons on the 1st floor of the house. It is dark in the staircase, but the goddess leads the way.

---

9. *Odyssey* 19: 33-43.

There are two quite distinct paragraphs, the second beginning with the temporal *dē tote* = "suddenly" in verse 35. The first paragraph is the end of the epic narrative I just referred to. The second paragraph is an account in direct speech. But it is the same event that is described in the two paragraphs.

In the first paragraph the divinity is described from the "Olympian", all-knowing, perspective in anthropomorphic terms: the divinity is identified as Pallas Athena, she is found in front of the heroes, and in her hand she is carrying "a golden lamp". The scenery is staged in a concrete way, and we get quite a visual experience of the goddess and the light from the lamp.

In the second paragraph Telemachus puts into words his experience of the presence of the goddess. But he can not see her, and he can not see any source of light: He can only see illuminated objects. He calls this event a "wonder" (*thauma*). He understands that a god is present, but he doesn't know who; only that "some god" (*tis theos*) is there.

Again, there seems to be a contrast between mythic narrative and "revelation" account, which is similar to the one we met in the old Egyptian texts: In the narrative texts the gods are vividly depicted, but the revelation texts' account is moderate and vague. They describe the effect of the god's presence, rather than the presence itself.

My purpose in this paper has been to pay attention to the fact that vital elements of religious life, such as the representations of gods, are conditioned by literary genre and speech situation. This raises a number of problems in comparative research. If the interrelationships between the representation of God (or any other religious element), linguistic form, and text genres, is a case of a more general phenomenon, this should have direct implications for phenomenological accounts of religious beliefs and attitudes. Continual attention must be given to variations conditioned by text-genre and context if we claim to describe a given type of concept or a group's or individual's notion of God. Certain literary categories may automatically imply fixed dimensions in the representation of God. When these dimensions appear to be functionally conditioned by the genre itself, the representation of God may be claimed to be a formal characteristic constitutive for the genre as such, rather than the expression of a generally comprised concept independent of genre.

## Bibliography

**Sources**
*The Odyssey* (The Loeb Classical Library). London 1960.
Urk IV = *Urkunden des ägyptischen Altertums. Bd. IV: Urkunden der 18. Dynastie.* Bearbeitet von Kurt Sethe. 2. Ausgabe. Leipzig-Berlin 1927-30.

**Secondary literature**
Assmann, Jan. 1977. "Gott." In W Helck – W Westendorf, eds., *Lexikon der Ägyptologie.* Band II. Wiesbaden. Pp. 756-786.
Ehnmark, Erland. 1935. *The Idea of God in Homer.* Uppsala.
–. 1939. *Anthropomorphism and Miracle.* Uppsala.
Hornung, Erik. 1973. *Der Eine und die Vielen. Ägyptische Gottesvorstellungen.* 2., unveränderter Auflage. Darmstadt.
Mayo, B. 1967. "Belief and Constraint." In A. Phillips Griffiths, ed., *Knowledge and Belief.* London.
Morenz, S. 1960. *Ägyptische Religion* (Die Religionen der Menschheit, Bd. 8), Stuttgart.
Needham, R. 1972. *Belief, Language and Experience.* Chicago.
Nilsson, Martin P. 1964. *A History of Greek Religion.* New York.
–. 1923/24. "Götter und Psychologie bei Homer." *Archiv für Religionswissenschaft* 22: 363-390.
Olsson, Tord. 1975-82. *Religious Documents of the Maasai* I-III, Lund.
–. 1984. "Gudsbild, talsituation och litterär genre. Exempel från maasaifolket i Kenya." *Föreningen Lärare i Religionskunskap. Årsbok 1983.* Årg 16.

# Reconceiving the Category of the Sacred

*William E. Paden*
UNIVERSITY OF VERMONT, USA

The venerable category of "the sacred"[1] has served as the central organizing concept of the phenomenology of religion since the turn of the century, and has had a busy though privileged career representing nothing less than the generic object of all religious expression. While some critics believe it is time for the word to retire, I would first rather explore the possibilities of re-contextualization and retooling. This paper reassesses the uses of the term when employed in a descriptive rather than theological, hegemonic context.

Critics allege that the term has been part of the language of a theological hermeneutic, that it implies an ontological referent, and that in general it is a religiously privileged category which cannot justify itself in the context of academic method.[2] The category of the sacred, including its influential Eliadean usages, is accused of being too much a synonym for divinity and too insinuative of its own existence as a religious reality to be appropriate for post-theological religious studies. In addition, the ahistorical use of the term is criticized for obscuring the contextual nature of religious life.

Since R.R. Marett's writings correlated it with mana, and Rudolf Otto linked it with the divine, the concept of "the sacred"

---

1. A useful, annotated, bibliographic survey of 146 books and articles about the concept of the sacred is Courtas and Isambert 1977.
2. For example, Penner 1990: 15-35, and Segal 1989.

or "the holy" has been used as a kind of epithet for the supernatural, i.e. a force that is mysteriously other, and which manifests itself in different objects in the world. This object-centered approach, or "mana model," became orthodoxy in the tradition of the phenomenology of religion.

The mana model served three ideologically useful functions. First, through the overarching concept of the sacred the reader of the encyclopedic phenomenologies was induced to see a unity amid the otherwise uncontrollable diversity of religious life. Second, that unity could be linked with the notion of a transcendent reality, "the sacred" being here synonymous with "the holy" (the German *das Heilige* collapses the distinction) and isomorphic with the divine. And third, apart from its quasi-philosophical appeal, the further attraction of this model was that it appeared to be a generous means for understanding symbol systems other than one's own, giving both intelligibility and dignity to the otherwise foreign concretizations of other peoples' religious lives. Thus religious people could be shown to be not really worshipping the literal object itself – the tree, the stone, the earth – but rather responding to "the sacred."

While this conceptual apparatus, with its totalizing nature, has become controversial, it is not clear that the category of sacredness *per se* needs to be abandoned. The option proposed here is to move the term towards a strictly descriptive function, with no referentialist frame, and in a way which brings together features of both anthropological and phenomenological perspective by linking the concept of the sacred with that of world construction. Rather than reifying the term as a name for the numinous, revelatory religious object, I propose "de-centralizing" it and investigating it as a class concept that designates a category of behaviors,[3] in line with recent moves toward

---

3. Comstock (1981) has also written along parallel lines, arguing that the sacred can be studied not just as an inner feeling-state, but a form of rule governed behavior. Where Comstock wishes to make the move from unobservables to observables, my concern here is with the even broader issue of theological vs. descriptive levels of analysis.

a more anthropologically adequate understanding of methodology.[4]

"Sacrality," indeed, is probably an even more serviceable word than "the sacred." "Sacral," "sacralization," and "sacrality" have been formed out of modern anthropological usage.[5] "Sacral" already has a descriptive, ethic nature, meaning "pertaining to religious rites or observances," and thus escapes some of the ambiguity of "the sacred," which has such strong emic or religious associations.

The essay first outlines a way of construing the descriptive object and function of the category, suggests recovering some of the Durkheimian contributions to this usage, then considers its uses as a conceptual, comparative tool, and finishes by identifying some of the issues and further prospects raised by this approach.

## Sacrality as a descriptive category

In religious studies the concept of the sacred has been so stretched by its invented, epithetical usage as a proper noun naming a spiritual force that it has lost its more straightforward value as a term describing a class of objects, a use observed by the Durkheimians. "Sacred," after all, is an adjective demarcating a type of relationship humans have to certain objects.[6] "Sacred" things are those dedicated or consecrated to a god or a religious purpose, and thus require behaviors which do not violate the status of those objects. This commonsense, nontechnical meaning calls attention to the way certain objects are constructed and committed by the actions of subjects, and it is in this way

---

4. For example, as represented in Tyloch 1990: 8.
5. Primarily over the last century, with a noticeable influence from the Durkheimian school. See the *Oxford English Dictionary*, 2d ed. For an extensive use of "sacrality", see Dupront 1987.
6. "Sacred" is the past participle of ME *sacren*, to consecrate, from OF *sacrer*, based on L. *sacrare*, and thus conveys a certain verbal (i.e. behavioral) meaning.

that sacredness can be taken not as a kind of substance or force, but as a category of behavior.

It might be productive to return to this basic behavioral and nonmetaphysical usage, and see what view sacrality yields when reconstructed inductively from comparative religious data. Most cultures have dedicated objects that are believed to be vehicles of supernatural life and which accordingly require specialized behaviors. Such objects include gods or spirit beings and their concrete symbols, certain places and times, certain persons or classes of persons, and ritual symbols, but also include laws and obligations, prayers and teachings, principles and precepts, bodies of authority, beliefs about one's identity, and states of mind. Durkheim's most common phrase for these was "sacred things," and from this notion came his class-concept nouns, "the sacred" and "sacredness."

If a sacred object is one constituted as such by the actions of subjects, then the actions of the believers and the objects of those actions form a single subject-object phenomenon. The behavioral component is an indispensable, constitutive factor in the equation.

From the point of view of an analysis of cultural behavior, sacredness is therefore both a way of actively constructing or focalizing the world and a way that objects face back to the insiders in that world.[7] Sacred things are formed (i.e. "dedicated") by society, in turn impose themselves back upon it with the force of their supposed objectivity, which object-like status in turn requires that the adherents act in a sacred manner.

Now cultural practices which are determined by the perceived sacrality of these objects can be understood as one *type* of system of behavior alongside others. Cultures contain several such systems, each forming a set of practices and rules appropriate to its objects and purposes. Any society has multiple behavioral languages such as games, courtship practices, and civic or

---

7. This relates to Jonathan Z. Smith's point that objects become sacred situationally, by virtue of the focalizing nature of ritual. (1987: 104).

military duties, and each of these will have a distinctive range of actions that fit the purposes of its subsystem. The quite different activities of a hockey game, a soccer game and chess game, each show a behavior that goes with the nature of their objects and goals. A religion, then, can be viewed as just such a system of behavior, one which organizes its language and practice around things that are deemed sacred.

Moreover, religious systems in turn involve any number of sacred objects within themselves. Thus, if the sacred object is a birth, a marriage, or a death, then the birth rite, marriage rite, and funeral rite may each involve a different set of behaviors. Within the progress of a single rite there can be an entire range of sacral subject/object moments, e.g. solemn or festive, penitential or celebratory. The multiple kinds of sacred objects create the multiple religious behaviors of the system, each responsive in a particular way to the particular nature of the object. A holy place is such an object, with attending behaviors, and a holy time (perhaps even conjoined with a holy place) is another; the wrathful "moment" of a god is such an object, the loving moment of the same god is another; what one's Church prescribes about abortion is such an object, and yet what one's conscience prescribes about it may be another.

Sacrality (or sacredness) would then be a class term used to mark off this cluster of behaviors characteristic of the structures and relationships by which people engage objects that have supernatural status, and religious systems will take innumerable historical and cultural forms according to the varying nature of the objects that are sacred and the varying styles of cultural behavior that form responses to those objects.

In this way sacrality is perceived not as an *a priori* for the historian of religion, but as a focal structure for the life of the religious insider and thus a category which points to and delineates the practices of the religious believers themselves. The data for the historian of religions are these worlds that are sacred to their own insiders, worlds which rise up around different sets of objects taken to be sacred.

Once this primary distinction is made clear, once it is clear that "the sacred" is not a name for the supernatural but for a category of behavior characteristic of religious insiders, then a certain methodological clarity is possible. For example, much of the controversy about Eliade's terminology derives both from his failure to make this distinction clear and the failure of his critics to see how very often his use of the term sacred refers either specifically or generically to what is sacred *for* the insider.

Because the historian of religion looks at the sacrality of these objects in terms of their function within their systems, sacredness will convey this element of relativity and contextuality rather than implying that each insider "participates" in a universal or archetypal experience of the supernatural or that the supernatural is "manifesting" itself in different systems. The Grand Shrine of Ise is not sacred to the Irish and the Shrine of the Black Madonna at Czestochowa, Poland, is not sacred to the Japanese. The Qur'an is not sacred to Buddhists, and Jews have little interest in the sacrality of the Ganges. Yet to the insider, sacred things are absolutes.[8]

## Sacrality as a descriptive category in the Durkheimian tradition

The concept of the sacred has not been limited to the classic religious phenomenologists. The Durkheimians, long ago, developed a non-theological use of the term, but because their terminology was wrapped in a sociological reduction, historians of religion have largely ignored or eschewed it. In rethinking a phenomenology of sacrality, it would be useful to return to some parts of the Durkheimian analysis,[9] while bracketing its

---

8. When Eliade speaks of the ontologies of religious peoples I usually interpret his language in that relativistic way, i.e. that it is *to the insider* that the sacred things are the most "real" things, charged with the greatest authority and power.
9. For an interesting attempt to construe Durkheim's approach to religion and sacrality as a rare blend of both *les sciences humaines* and *les sciences religieuses*, see Prades 1987.

causalistic framework. *The Elementary Forms of the Religious Life* offers several distinctions which are suggestive for this project, points I will only briefly epitomize here.[10]

The Durkheimian model of sacrality represents quite a different program than that of the supernaturalist paradigms of scholars like Marett, Söderblom, Lehmann, Otto, and van der Leeuw. In the *Elementary Forms* Durkheim does *not* use the concept of the sacred to denote the supernatural object of religion, but rather to describe a particular system of behavior. Sacred things are objects kept from profanization. Here the "sacred" is *not* synonymous with a mysterious, transcendental, or wholly other force, with power or with mana. It is not a metaphysical object at all, and certainly not divinity or something that "manifests" itself.

Durkheim does think there is such a force, and labels it "the totemic principle," but he does not semantically identify or confuse it with "the sacred." He distinguishes the *source* of the sacred, i.e. the power of collective authority, from the behavior of sacredness. What phenomenologists called "the sacred/holy" Durkheim called the totemic principle.[11] Semantically and structurally Durkheim's *le sacré* belongs to a different theoretic universe than Otto's *das Heilige*, and refers to different sets of data.

Durkheim treats sacrality in two different and alternating discursive contexts: the descriptive and the explanatory. In the first, he is concerned to establish and describe the *existence* of religious facts or phenomena. Sacredness, and the distinction of sacred and profane states are such facts, part of the peculiar nature of religious data. They are different in kind than other behaviors and symbol systems and they have their own logic.[12]

---

10. For a more detailed account of these points see Paden 1991, an article from which I draw certain formulations here.
11. Evidently neither could speak of this religious "force" (read: "source") without an act of foundationalist annexation.
12. Even in his early writings (e.g. his 1899 essay on the definition of religious phenomena) Durkheim stressed that sacredness *per se* was a category "irreducible to any other group of phenomena" (Durkheim 1975: 88).

Only at the second, causalistic, level does Durkheim then try to *explain* the existence of the sacredness by showing its origins in the chemistry of collective power and identity. His method, then, is first to describe religion, then explain it; first depict the nature of religious experience, and then analyze the reality underlying it.

This is to suggest that the descriptive value of Durkheim's vocabulary may be useful on its own, even apart from his sociological conclusions. For example, his careful analysis of the interplay of sacred and profane states in the activity of asceticism is one discourse (Durkheim 1965: 348-355); but his final *explanation* of ascetic renunciation in terms of the subordination of individuality to social ideals is another (356). The same distinction of description ("of natural classes of facts") and analytic explanation is present in works like the essay on sacrifice (1898) by Hubert and Mauss and Mauss's study of the nature of magic (1904).

Moreover, in speaking of sacredness Durkheim is obviously and exclusively referring to what is sacred *for* the insider. Sacrality is *a priori* not for the interpreter, but for the participants, who configure their world and behaviors as responses to sacred objects.

Durkheim's statements about all religious worlds being divided into sacred and profane realms (Durkheim 1965: 52-56) has indeed served to confuse the issue of his relevance. Anthropologists state that they find no such dualism in their field work, typically reporting that they see a fusion of sacred and secular realms more often than a separation.[13] Yet it remains that in spite of this representational dualism Durkheim is quite clear about the fluidity or transformational character of sacred and profane in the realm of ritual practice, where the profane *state* can become sacred through the metamorphic force of purification and where the very purpose of ritual is to link sacred and profane realms (Durkheim 1965: 348ff., 380). Indeed, society itself can "constantly create sacred things out of ordinary ones"

---

13. For a summary of criticisms of Durkheim's idea of the sacred/profane polarity see Pickering 1984: 115-162.

(243). Sacred and profane here refer not just to objects, but also to states that are changeable.

If he was overzealous and ambiguous in the definition of dualistic realms of representation,[14] Durkheim was more careful in his analysis of how sacred and profane objects and states are ritually negotiated by the participants. He transforms the concept of taboo into the larger notion of incompatibility. Sacred and profane states are those which cannot coexist at the same time, and from an understanding of the logic of this incongruity, not from sociological analysis per se, he unfolds a rationale for the dynamics of religious behavior and the transformational process of de-profanization. "A man cannot approach his god intimately while he still bears on him marks of his profane life," and one approaches the sacred "by the very act of leaving the profane" (Durkheim 1965: 346, 348). This goes beyond the simplistic Frazerian idea that sacred things are just untouchable, tabooed things, by also developing the inverse concept that it is the profane things/states which must be avoided or abstained from in order to maintain states of sanctity (342-347). In Durkheim's hands interdiction ceases to represent savage ignorance or negative magic and becomes a basic system of the logic of purity and impurity, thus paving the way for the work of Mary Douglas and Louis Dumont.

Significantly, in this version of sacrality, the "profane" does not just mean the mundane or natural world, as it does for Eliade, but that which violates or is actively incompatible with the sacred.[15] The latter is what must be kept from sacrilege. It is not

---

14. I attribute this to 1) the overriding way in which taboo served for him as an initial model of sacrality, 2) his absolute commitment to the dualistic character of collective vs. individual modes of thought, and 3) his failure in this case to distinguish between sacred/profane as fixed realms and sacred/profane as relationships *to* things.

15. Though he is inconsistent on this. Durkheim elsewhere uses what might be called a version of the mana model when he contrasts the ecstatic experience of collective events with the banality of individual life and presents that distinction as the origin of the sacred/profane polarity (1965: 245-250). In this sense, the *Elementary Forms* contains more than one model of sacrality.

101

simply a cipher for the transcendent. So the process of how religious people deal with profanity in all its forms (e.g. religious court cases) becomes here an inexhaustible phenomenon for study, whereas the mana model focuses almost solely and statically on the apprehension of the numinous object *per se*.

## Uses of the category of sacrality

A concept of sacrality can identify and illumine the way a specific kind of cultural system shapes human experience according to its own categories and reference points, and it can do this without foreclosing on metaphysical issues. It becomes an instrument for understanding world formation, drawing attention to the actual objects around which someone else's world forms. The behavior of others becomes intelligible when seen as a response to those objects, and to miss the role of the objects is to miss the point of the behavior.

More specifically, the category of sacrality can show the relative power that sacred objects have to shape the nature of authority, cosmology, social values and selfhood. While religious objects (e.g. belief in a deity) can represent a weak system of world-shaping, relative to other or secular systems of culture, they can also represent a strong system of world construction where relatively extensive areas of personal and social life are brought under their domain – extreme examples being monasteries or communitarian religious groups. Sacred systems thus can create their own version of social order. They can create hierarchy but also democracy, this-worldly or other-worldly values, rigid social stratification but also liminality and its dismantling of roles and structures.

The experience of sacred objects is of course not monolithic, but creates different forms of behavior. Particular theories of the sacred have seized on one or another of these genres and made it the single, thematic model for sacrality in general, e.g. Otto's "sense of the numinous," Eliade "opening to the transcendent," van der Leeuw's "response to power," and Tillich's "ultimate concern." Even Durkheim's overemphasis on sacredness as that which is separated or tabooed was a limitation to his own system.[16] But sacred objects elicit a whole range of relationships, and a descriptive, pluralistic approach to sacrality will take account of all of them. For example, the phenomenon of "otherness," rather than being reified and asserted as the sole paradigm of sacrality – as in the Protestant Christian schemas of Otto and van der Leeuw – becomes one among several of its features. Sacred objects can have imposing objective attributes, and can present themselves as mysterious, daunting, miraculous, and filled with mana, but such numinous otherness is only one segment of the range of object-relationships. It is equally important in studying religion to see the sacrality of *dharma* and *sharia*, of law and tradition, of obligation and bonding.

## The category of sacrality as comparative tool

This revised notion of sacredness may be accompanied by a restated notion of its relation to comparative method.[17] Comparative perspective here looks at analogies and differences in the way sacrality structures worlds, rather than at the way generic acts and symbols show universal human "responses to the Sacred." It aims to understand both what is common and what is specific in any religious expression.

Uncovering the thematic, typological structures of sacrality provides an intercultural frame of reference for understanding phenomena which might otherwise remain obscure, undervalued or miscontextualized. Familiarity with a large, cross-cultural range of sacred objects and their functions creates a categorial background that can be useful in approaching new religious data. While the specific meanings of sacred objects to insiders

---

16. It is ironic that Durkheim, the great sociologue, did not develop an analysis of the sacrality of bonding, loyalty and allegiance.
17. For a full length study of such a readjusted comparative program, linking the anthropological acknowledgment of cultural specificity with the intercontextual, phenomenological analysis of analogous structures, see Paden 1988.

are not accounted for in any general concepts of sacredness, the latter nevertheless might help an historian of religion find intelligibility in the overall religious functions of the insider's culture-specific symbols and behaviors. If one is familiar with "center of the world" sacralities, the insider's claim that a certain volcano or mountain is the navel of the universe will appear less strange. Outsiders who do not see the role of the sacred or the logics of its subcategorical forms (e.g. sacrifice, mythic time, asceticism, sacred times, sacred kingship) in the behavior of religious insiders, or who have no notion of how relationships to sacred objects form distinctive shapings of behavior and world, will automatically supply their own categories of interpretation, which may have nothing to do with the phenomenon. By analogy, a person who knows music generally may have a better chance of making sense of otherwise foreign musical expressions.

At the same time, comparative work does not just provide typological understanding, but through building up a sense of what is behaviorally common, directs attention also to what is different. Without seeing what is common one cannot see what is different. Things are "different" in relation *to* a common theme, so that identifying common ways that sacred objects structure worlds *leads* to the question of the different ways these objects function and their difference in content. A pilgrimage to Mecca is not the same thing as a pilgrimage to Benares. The differences are important and interesting. The same pilgrimage may even "mean" different things to the same person at different times. Likewise, gods – as types of sacred objects – differ in nature and function, just as the same god may differ in nature and function at different times. Religious history thus represents not just the repetition of the same themes, but their cultural recreation in a sequence of ever new versions of sacrality. In this way the comparative study of sacrality, while generalizing *from* historical material, then faces back to history and its varieties, developments, and specific sociocultural contexts.

The objects that are taken as sacred comprise a story of diversity. In historical religions one type of sacrality often replaces a previous one. Buddhist monasticism created a new system of sacred principles over against Brahmanism. But later forms of Japanese Buddhism protested against the values of monasticism, creating lay movements which focused on the power of faith and its this-worldly applications. In Europe, Protestant groups replaced cultic, hieratic and priestly sacrality with personal regeneration through "the Word." Pulpits replaced altars as sacral foci. The Durkheimians themselves were intrigued by the evolution of "the sacred character of the human person" and the emergence of the sacrality of human rights in modern societies.[18]

Two or more religious expressions may share some features of sacrality in common, yet this does not imply that they "mean" the same thing. The consecrated Christian host, the Australian aboriginal *churinga*, and the Soka Gakkai *gohonzon* have some analogous functions in terms of their ritual holiness and focalizing nature, but this does not imply that they have the same meaning, since meaning is intimately connected with their respective differences of mythological/cultural context. Here "meaning" specifically signifies meaning to the insider, and what the themes of sacrality signify to the comparativist is still an altogether different matter.

Comparative knowledge and local knowledge are not exclusive alternatives but complement each other. On the one hand, no cultural expression is completely unique, as it will always have something in common with other things, but on the other hand there is also no thing which does not have a unique aspect, given its contextualization in time, space and culture. Thus, comparative work becomes the developed understanding of analogy and difference based on the greatest possible set of religious worlds, an approach which does not replace single-system, ethnographic analysis, but rather works in conjunction with it.

---

18. For example, Mauss 1979, 90; and for a review of the issue, see Pickering 1984: 476-499.

WILLIAM E. PADEN

# An integral phenomenology of sacrality: some implications

In conclusion, I would mention a few factors that seem implicated in this refocusing of the category.

(1) The issue of whether the sacred is or is not an irreducible or *sui generis* religious category[19] begins to be sorted out. Sacrality is not an *a priori* category that insinuates a religious reality, but is a thematic construct which draws attention to certain forms of behavior and may help in the exploration of the structure of religious life. It is a category of culture and society, yet, like music, science and games, is a form of activity and classification with its own typical ways of shaping the world. The "irreducibility of the sacred," then, need not be a banner for religious privilege, but simply a signpost for investigating a distinct type of cultural experience.

Nor does this concept presuppose an exclusive opposition between "social" and "religious." As a form of behavior, the phenomenon of sacrality is open to either religious or sociological interpretation or both.[20]

(2) If the concept of sacredness is here not just a label for the transcendent, then more attention is drawn to its linkages with the phenomena of order, boundaries, law and authority, i.e. to its interaction with categories of social structure. What presents itself as a sacred object, after all, can also be viewed as a sociopolitical object, just as the same object can function simultaneously in more than one system of reference. For example, as a collective phenomenon, supernaturally legitimated sacred order will automatically carry the weight, values and function of a social order. The vitality and absoluteness of sacred objects are thus enhanced and underscored by the fact that the existence of the group is at stake in the maintenance of those objects, so

---

19. See Pals, Segal, and Wiebe 1991.
20. Of course the plot thickens here. For a study of the issue of how interpretive frames select their own data, see Paden 1992.

that sacred things are not only a category of revelation (i.e. to the insider) but also a specific function of the authority of the collective system. The supernatural object and the system of collective order reinforce each other and guarantee each other's reality.[21]

Yet if sacred objects can function as condensed representations of the identity of the group itself, it is not necessary to adopt Durkheim's sociological causalism to acknowledge the way in which the phenomenology of the sacred follows sociocultural contours, or even the way, in Durkheimian vocabulary, in which the totemic symbol is "the very type of sacred thing" (Durkheim 1965: 140).

(3) De-theologized, the category of sacrality also brings questions about its more sinister sides, i.e. its connection with violence, intolerance and exclusion, authoritarianism, socioreligious wars and purges. Sacred objects are not only links to another world, but forces which create divisions and role discrimination in this one. History continues to record dark instances of the use of supernatural legitimation for raw political self-interest. Sacrality can be raw or cooked.

If religious and social world-making operate in close alliance, then the category of sacrality becomes not just a nice blanket term for a sublime cosmic reality, but a truly neutral term that can have any content. If the phenomenology of the sacred can provide material for doing theology, it can also provide material, ultimately, for doing social criticism.

(4) Without their epistemic overlays, the phenomenological structures of Eliade and Durkheim even have a certain complementary continuity. While this is not the place to argue it, I would suggest that Eliade's relation to the constructivist categories of the French school is much closer than has been acknowledged, and that the study of Eliade's French connection will illumine our understanding of both Eliade and the Durkheimians.

---

21. A point discussed by Isambert 1982: 270.

In any case, in none of the features of this analysis is the category of sacrality a hidden theology. And while I cannot argue that this concept is indispensable for studying religion, it is still not yet clear what will replace it, and it does at least seem to have its heuristic and educational uses in the current fashioning of secular maps of knowledge.

## Bibliography

Comstock, W. Richard. 1981. "A Behavioral Approach to the Sacred: Category Formation in Religious Studies." *Journal of the American Academy of Religion* XLIX (4): 625-643.

Courtas, Raymonde and F.-A. Isambert. 1977. "La Notion de 'Sacré:' Bibliographie thématique." *Archives de Sciences sociales des Religions* 44 (1): 119-138.

Dupront, Alphonse. 1987. *Du Sacré: Croisades et pèlerinages, Images et langages.* Paris.

Durkheim, Emile. 1965. *The Elementary Forms of the Religious Life.* Trans. Joseph Ward Swain. New York.

–. 1975. "Concerning the Definition of Religious Phenomena." In W.S.F. Pickering, *Durkheim on Religion: A Selection of Readings with Bibliographies.* Trans. Jacqueline Redding and W.S.F. Pickering. London.

Isambert, François-André. 1982. *Le Sens du Sacré: fête et religion populaire.* Paris.

Mauss, Marcel. 1979. *Sociology and Psychology: Essays.* Trans. Ben Brewster. London.

Paden, William E. 1988. *Religious Worlds: The Comparative Study of Religion.* Boston.

–. 1991. "Before 'The Sacred' Became Theological: Rereading the Durkheimian Legacy." *Method and Theory in the Study of Religion* 3 (1): 10-23.

–. 1992. *Interpreting the Sacred: Ways of Viewing Religion.* Boston.

Pals, Daniel L., Robert A. Segal and Donald Wiebe. 1991. "Axioms Without Dogmas." *Journal of the American Academy of Religion* LIX (4): 703-712.

Penner, Hans H. 1990. *Impasse and Resolution: A Critique of the Study of Religion.* New York.

Pickering, W.S.F. 1984. *Durkheim's Sociology of Religion: Themes and Theories.* London.

Prades, José A. 1987. *Persistance et métamorphose du sacré: actualiser Durkheim et repenser la modernité.* Paris.

Segal, Robert A. 1989. *Religion and the Social Sciences: Essays on the Confrontation.* Brown Studies in Reigion, no. 3. Atlanta, Georgia.

Smith, Jonathan Z. 1987. *To Take Place: Toward Theory in Ritual.* Chicago.

Tyloch, Witold, ed. 1990. *Studies on Religions in the Context of Social Sciences. Methodological and Theoretical Relations.* Polish Society for the Science of Religions. Warsaw.

# Comparative Religion: Between Phenomenology and Typology of Religions

*Erik Reenberg Sand*
UNIVERSITY OF COPENHAGEN, DENMARK

## Introduction

Before beginning the present paper, it is my duty to state that not all of what I am going to say is new. In fact much of it is rooted in the viewpoints of the comparative religion of the beginning of this century, and, to be more specific, I have drawn inspiration from the grand old man of Danish history of religions, Vilhelm Grønbech, of whom I have made a renewed study within the last couple of years.[1]

However, it is my belief that we should not always uncritically throw away what is old and look to everything that is new, just because it is new. Often one may, in fact, find inspiration in the past history of our discipline with regard to methods and theories which have been discarded, but may show themselves to answer some of our present problems and challenges.

## Historical and phenomenological approaches to the study of religions

It is no secret that one of the most debated issues within the history of religions since the last world war has involved the competing claims of historical and phenomenological approaches

---

1. Cp. Sand 1991.

to the study of religion.[2] This debate has been the object of several conferences, and has been explained in several ways, both as a "breach between scholars of different inclinations and temperaments" (Sharpe), and as a competition between various methods within the history of religions. No doubt different temperaments have something to do with it, even though this observation does not free us from taking the discussion seriously if we want to call the history of religions a science. But to see the rivalry between "historians" and "phenomenologists" as a tension between different methods seems to me highly questionable, since both parts in the debate, I am sure, would readily subscribe to the indispensability of the historical-philological method, as well as other methods such as field-work methods, archaeological methods etc. Rather, the differences have to do with the aims of the study of religion and with the fact that "historians" and "phenomenologists" are working on different levels of explanation.

Thus, the chief aim of the historically minded scholar is to study individual religions both synchronically, as harmonious structures of various religious forms such as rituals, myths, ethics, religious conceptions etc., and diachronically in order to find out how and why these structures develop through time. Furthermore, he may also concentrate on the influences which the religion under study has received from or effected on other religions or cultures. To pursue these goals he may adopt a range of different methods and perspectives, historical and hermeneutic. Whether he works on the synchronic or diachronic level, he is generally attentive to the relations between so-called religious and other cultural and social phenomena, because the latter are crucially important for an understanding of most major changes in religious structures. To the historically minded scholar religion, culture, and society are inseparable.

The phenomenologically minded scholar, on the other hand,

---

2. For surveys of this discussion, see Sharpe 1975: 220-250, and 278 ff., and, especially, King 1984: 29-164.

has as his chief aim to study in a cross-cultural manner the different forms individual religious phenomena take in different religions, such as rituals, myths, the concepts of gods, death etc. The phenomenological approach may be carried out on different levels. On one hand we have restricted attempts to deal separately with single religious phenomena, either in the form of monographs or articles. On the other hand we have the much more ambitious and general "phenomenologies" in which a single scholar tries to encompass all religious phenomena or perhaps one should rather say the whole phenomenon of religion, in the singular. Here one may mention the works of Gerardus van der Leeuw, Friedrich Heiler, Gustav Mensching, William Brede Kristensen, and Geo Widengren. Due to the fact that fewer and fewer scholars today have the capacity to deal with such vast material, and perhaps also because standards have changed, the more modest restricted phenomenological approach seems to be gaining ground while the more audacious general attempt has fallen into desuetude. Restricted phenomenology seems to have become particularly favored as a means to generate themes for the seminars and symposia that gather together religious scholars with widely separate areas of specialization, who may have, perhaps, nothing else to talk about.

I just mentioned that the differences between the historical and the phenomenological approach to the study of religion have less to do with differences of method than with differences of the aim of the study and the different levels of explanation. Thus, we may say that the restricted phenomenological approach positions itself at a sort of meta-level in relation to specific historic researches. By using the results of work done on the historical level, it seeks to compare, systematize, and classify separate, religious phenomena. And again, with regard to the general phenomenology of van der Leeuw and others, we may say that they function on an even higher and abstract meta-meta-level in relation to restricted phenomenology, often appropriating the results of this more modest approach for its own purposes.

With regard to the differences of aim of the study, it is, I think, obvious that many phenomenologists do not restrict themselves to a purely historical interest in religious phenomena, but rather seem to be led by more philosophical or even theological intentions. Although this is rarely explicit, it is most evident with the so-called "classical" school of phenomenology of van der Leeuw and Friedrich Heiler. This school works from the almost Platonic starting point that the phenomena are manifestations of an *Essenz* or *Wesen* which may be perceived by the scholar by the help of an intuitive process in which the concept *epoché*, or "Einklammerung", plays an important role. Thus, this kind of phenomenology is closely interwoven with hermeneutical ideas, going back to the religio-philosophical thought of the German Protestant theology of Friedrich Schleiermacher, which, if they give any sense at all as methodological concepts, are much more appropriate on the level of historical-philological research than on the meta-level of phenomenology. Clearly the overall aim of this school of phenomenology of religion is to look behind the historical, religious phenomena to posit a supposed essence behind them: Religion with a capital R. It is thus contrary to the aims of most religio-historical research. In this religio-philosophical or theological light it also seems clear that the concept of *epoché* is more a defensive concept employed by van der Leeuw and his disciples to distance themselves from purely confessional research than it is a strictly methodological device.

Unfortunately, this "essence" thinking of the general phenomenological school manifests itself in the way most of their works structure religious phenomena, with the concept of the divine at the centre as the object of all religious aspiration and behaviour. This is perhaps most evident in the large work of Friedrich Heiler: *Erscheinungsformen und Wesen der Religion* in which he describes his approach as an approach of concentric circles ("konzentrischen Kreise"), in which the "secret god" (deus absconditus) is at the centre, while in the outer circles we find first religious concepts and then religious acts.[3] Here it is

---

3. Cp. Heiler 1961: 19 ff.

obvious to anyone that we are dealing not with a religio-historical method, but with a religio-philosophical or theological way of organizing the religious phenomena according to the world view of Western Christianity, and mainly Protestant tradition. Thus, it would be a gross misconception of many primitive and antique religions to speak of god as being at the center of their religion.

In some respects, the so-called "hermeneutical" school of Mircea Eliade, which through its ancestors, Joachim Wach and Rudolf Otto, stands in a kind of cousin-relationship with classical phenomenology, is susceptible to the same critique, though these authors do not speak about the secret god, but about the more neutral "the sacred". On the other hand, this school has perhaps another weak point in its marked tendency towards symbolism, which sometimes tends to give a little too low priority to the ritual side of most religions.

Thus, in the case of the general "phenomenologies" of, say, a van der Leeuw, Heiler, Mensching, or Brede Kristensen, the way they structure religious phenomena is so far removed from historical facts that their approach seems not a science, but more of an art or a religio-philosophy for liberal Christian theologians that reflects a Christian concept of religion.

Clearly the more modest, restricted phenomenology is not to the same extent susceptible to this critique. But I am still afraid that on a lesser scale it often runs the same risk of inattention to the position the phenomena under study have in the structure of their respective religion or culture, which produces distortions and misinterpretations. To give an example, one can note the different concepts of the divine in a so-called primitive religion and in Christianity, but this tells us nothing about the relative importance and position of divinity in the two cultures. Distortions also follow when phenomenologists note the existence of a given item in some religions, but ignore its equally important non-existence in others. This is the case, for instance, with many ideas about death and eschatology which we normally find only at a later stage in religious development. Quite often, phenomenology, as actually practiced, functions only as a kind of curiosity collection, which gives a somewhat flattened picture of religious reality, and most often from a Christian point of view.

Furthermore, it seems that restricted phenomenology is in need of an explanation of what it is actually doing when it lifts a religious phenomenon out of its historical, cultural, and social context, in order to compare it with similar phenomena in a totally different culture or in an altogether different age. Is this procedure not based on the same assumption as that of general phenomenology where religion is something in itself, something universal that manifests itself in man, in *homo religiosus*, and which may therefore be studied regardless of time and space? And is this approach not equally dangerous as in general phenomenology, in the sense that it disregards the position that the phenomena under study have in the specific, overall structure of the religion from which they are taken? Only it is not so visible here as in the case of general phenomenology.[4]

What within the human sciences we call religion is not a self existing, metaphysical category, but a culturally defined concept covering a group of phenomena that may all likewise be called either cultural, social, historical, or psychological. Therefore, these phenomena should not be studied as something existing outside of these contexts, unless we are given a good reason for doing so. Most present phenomenology of religion, so at least it seems to me, does not pay sufficient attention to the context of the studied religious phenomena. Therefore it is even more susceptible to the fact that we still do not, and probably never will agree, upon a definition of religion.

Notwithstanding this criticism of the phenomenology of reli-

---

4. For a similar discussion, see already Durkheim's critique of the British anthropological school which he critizises for trying to "go beyond the national and historical differences to the universal and really human bases of the religious life" (Durkheim 1971: 93). Here one may also refer to Radcliffe-Brown's observation that what appears to be the same social usage in two societies may have different functions in the two (Radcliffe-Brown 1952: 184).

gion, I will readily admit that comparison is an inherent element in the history of religions, as it is in all human sciences which aim to understand other persons or cultures, whether it be literary studies, historical sciences, or psychology. It is simply not possible to understand our fellow human beings without comparing at least with ourselves, or with our own culture.[5] And especially for a historian of religions, who normally studies several religions, the historical and comparative aspects are necessarily intertwined, since he can not help using knowledge obtained from the study of e.g. ritual in one religion when he studies ritual in another. Only he does not always make these processes clear to himself.

Therefore, the problem of the relationship and relative value of the phenomenological and the historical approach within the history of religions is not a question of either/or, but one of balance: To which approach do you attach the greatest importance? I find that the comparative element should continue to be handmaid of, and subordinate to, the historical study, especially as its procedures and raison d'être are still not clear and undisputed. Furthermore, I think we must either clarify the role and strategies of phenomenology in the study of religion, or accept that this is not possible, in which case it would perhaps be better to agree that phenomenology of religion is not a science but a sub-discipline within the history of religions useful chiefly for issues of classification and nomenclature. Its place in our curricula would then first of all be as a kind of propaedeutic discipline suitable for introducing beginners to the terminology of the history of religions, as well as giving them some representative examples of the various phenomena.

## Typology of religions: The third approach

I should, however, like to give some preliminary suggestions about the way I think, we might renew phenomenology of reli-

---

5. Cp. Lanczkowski 1978: 1 ff.

gions and make it more attentive to the cultural, historical, and sociological aspects of religious phenomena.[6]

What I am thinking of is the possibility of combining restricted phenomenology, understood as the cross-cultural study of separate religious phenomena, with a third approach to the study of religions, namely the approach normally called the typology of religions. In some ways this approach occupies an intermediate position between the historical and the phenomenological. Thus it is historical in the sense that it deals with cultures as wholes, taking into consideration their internal structure, and comparative in the sense that instead of comparing single phenomena cross-culturally, it compares entire cultures with a similar religious structure and a similar sociological and economical background.[7]

This would, I think, give us a more systematic means of assuring that, even though we study a single phenomenon, we draw our attention both to its position in the overall structure of the various religions from which we take our examples, and to its relations with the rest of the culture and society.

Thus every time we deal with a certain phenomenon we would have to treat its position in a number of chosen types of religion. And these types would have to be more or less the same for every phenomenon that we choose to study. In that way we would, perhaps, get a clearer and more historically based phenomenology on the one hand, and on the other hand our phenomenological studies would be subordinate to and would help investigate the value of our typology or typologies.

---

6. Another way, would be to limit the area of research to regions where the researcher has the greatest possible acquaintance with the sources. This is the procedure recommended by Åke Hultkrantz (1970). This would, of course, be an advantage especially in bringing forth empirical research of greater value for phenomenological studies. However, it does not in itself give us any clue as to the way these studies should be conducted.
7. Heiler calls this approach the approach of the "Querschnitte" as opposed to the approach of the "Längdeschnitte" or historical study and the approach of the "konzentrischen Kreise" which is his name for phenomenology (1961: 18 f.).

The major difficulty in this connection is, however, that unfortunately there exists no agreement among scholars with regard to the criteria according to which such a typology should be built. If we look at the various typologies that have been produced, we find that they have been made according to sociological, geographical, psychological, phenomenological, and ecological criteria. Thus, as examples built upon sociological and geographical criteria, we have the distinction between national and universal religions,[8] between primitive religions, the so-called peoples' religions, and world religions,[9] between tribes-, peoples-, national-, and universal religions,[10] or between primitive and urban religions.[11] As examples of typologies built upon phenomenological criteria we have various distinctions according to animism, preanimism, polytheism, henotheism, dualism, monotheism and pantheism. As an example of a typology built on philosophical or hermeneutical principles we may mention the distinction between religions of nature and religions of culture.[12] And as examples of typologies on a psychological basis we may mention Söderblom's distinction between religion as method, as psychology, as love of god, as salvation, as fight against evil, as good conscience, and as revelation.[13] In this connection we may also mention the typologies found in the phenomenologies of van der Leeuw and Mensching which are likewise mainly build upon a psychological basis.[14] Finally, we also meet with typologies that mix the various criteria, to mention only one example: the distinction between religions of nature, ethical religions, and universal religions.[15] Finally, we may also, I

---

8. Cp. Kuenen 1882.
9. Cp. Th. Steinmann 1913-14.
10. Heiler 1961: 19.
11. Cp. Pallis 1926: 269 ff., and 1959.
12. Cp. Tiele 1912.
13. Cp. Söderblom 1933: 67.
14. It is noteworthy that here these typologies function only as a kind of appendix, but are not an integral part of the phenomenologies as such.
15. Tiele 1912.

think, in this connection mention ecological typology as suggested by Åke Hultkrantz, on inspiration from the work of Julian Steward.[16]

Now, as is probably obvious from the just mentioned examples some typologies base their criteria on facts which lie outside of the phenomena that we call religious. This is first of all the case with typologies based on sociological, geographical, and ecological criteria, but is also to some extent valid for the distinction according to nature and culture. In comparison, phenomenologically and psychologically based typologies are usually defined according to criteria within the phenomena we call religious, which has the serious disadvantage that most of these typologies use categories that are themselves the results of earlier scholarly attempts to characterize the different religions. Typology of this sort can thus be circular, as well as rigid and static, resistant to further adjustments. First of all it is unable to satisfy the demand that any comparative exercise should respect the whole structure of the religion under investigation. This is most obvious with typologies based on various concepts of the divine, as these, as I have already observed, imply that the divine stands at the center of all religions as in the case of our own Christian religion. With regard to psychological typologies, these have the disadvantage that they focus too much on the personal attitude, which again is not representative of many non-Christian religions more rooted in collective experience.

In order to build up the best conceivable typology, which would make it possible to study religious phenomena in their relation to other social and cultural features, I therefore suggest it is necessary to base it on criteria that are outside what we normally call religious. Only in this way will we be able to pay full attention to the religious structure, as well as to those phenomena. Although, I have no time here to argue for a specific and detailed typology, such a typology would in my view have to be based on sociological and perhaps also ecological criteria in or-

---

16. Cp. Hultkrantz 1966.

der to take into account the influence of various types of social organization and occupation.

Roughly speaking it should incorporate some "primitive" religions and religions of antiquity, where, as has been done by Vernant e.g., we should perhaps have to distinguish between the religions of the Greek and Roman *polis* on the one hand,[17] and the religions of Egypt and Mesopotamia, which are based upon a more centrally governed political system, on the other.[18] Common to both of these categories is that they are national or ethnic. We should also include religions of more universal nature, which may or may not be ethnic in character. All of these are characterized by being based on a much more complicated social, economic, and political organization, and by a resulting individualization. Among these we have of course the five so-called world religions, and as special sub-type, the religious systems of late Antiquity or Hellenistic times. With regard to the use of ecological criteria, it seems to me that this mainly gives sense as a classificatory instrument, when we deal with so-called primitive religions, where dependence upon nature is especially heavy, and thus may be used as a means of further classification according to livelihood and occupation.[19]

---

17. Cp. Vernant 1962, and later works.
18. Cp. also Gernet 1932, which distinguishes between "le système de l'époque classique" and "l'universalisme".
19. For a relatively recent attempt to use ecology as basis for comparison, see Lincoln 1981.

# Bibliography

Durkheim, Emile. 1971. *The Elementary Forms of the Religious Life*. London.
Gernet, Louis. 1932. *Le génie grec dans la religion*. Paris.
Heiler, Friedrich. 1961. *Erscheinungsformen und Wesen der Religion*. Stuttgart.
Hultkrantz, Åke. 1966. "An Ecological Approach to Religion." *Ethnos* 31: 131-150.
–. 1970. "The Phenomenology of Religions: Aims and Methods." *Temenos* 6: 68-88.
King, Ursula. 1984. "Historical and Phenomenological Approaches to the Study of Religion: Some major developments and issues under debate since 1950." In Frank Whaling, ed., *Contemporary Approaches to the Study of Religion*. Vol I. The Hague.
Kuenen, A. 1882. *National Religions and Universal Religions*. London and Edinburgh (= The Hibbert Lectures, 1882).
Lanczkowski, Günter. 1978. *Einführung in die Religionsphänomenologie*. Darmstadt.
Lincoln, Bruce. 1981. *Priests, Warriors, and Cattle: A Study in the Ecology of Religions*. Berkeley.
Pallis, Svend Aage. 1926. *The Babylonian Akitu Festival*. Copenhagen (= Det Kgl. Danske Videnskabernes Selskab. Historisk-filologiske Meddelelser XII, 1).
–. 1959. "Idées fondamentales de l'étude des religions." *Numen* 6: 157-174.
Radcliffe-Brown, A. 1952. "On the concept of function in social science." In *Structure and Function in Primitive Society*, London.
Sand, Erik Reenberg. 1991. "Vilhelm Grønbech som sammenlignende religionshistoriker: Nogle perspektiver belyst ud fra hans forelæsningsrække om Religiøse Typer fra 1919." *Chaos, Dansk- Norsk Tidsskrift for Religionshistoriske Studier* 15: 25-53.
Sharpe, Eric J. 1975. *Comparative Religion: A History*, London.
Söderblom, Nathan. 1933. *The Living God*, Oxford.
Steinmann, Th. 1913-14. "Stufenfolge der Religionen." In *Religion Geschichte und Gegenwart*. Band 5. Tübingen.
Tiele, C. P. 1912. *Kompendium der Religionsgeschichte*. Vierte völlig umgearbeitete Auflage von D, Nathan Söderblom. Berlin.
Vernant, Jean-Pierre. 1962. *Les origines de la pensée grecque*. Paris.

# Typological and Genetic Comparisons: Implications and Perspectives

*Jens Peter Schjødt*
UNIVERSITY OF AARHUS, DENMARK

The scope of this paper is to discuss the limits and possibilities of different types of comparison used in the study of religion, in connection with semantic analysis. To be more specific, my aim is to discuss the methodological consequences of the fact that religions all over the world show great similarity in morphology as well as content. And to be even more specific, the question is: how do we handle situations where comparisons can shed light on a religion of which we know certain expressions, textual or pictorial, but do not have sufficient material for evaluating the semantic content of the expressions. This is, of course, especially the case in connection with so-called "dead" religions.

Comparison involves establishing differences as well as similarities.[1] Although one could compare religions with an eye to the differences, most comparisons remain chiefly concerned with similarities, at least as a basis for also noticing differences. For instance it is merely trivial to note that the concept "the other" is different in classical Greece and in the Old Testament: polytheism vs. monotheism, anthropomorphism vs. nonanthropomorphism etc.; whereas the differences between Allah and Jahve are more instructive, precisely because these figures are so similar in other ways.

One way or another, comparisons are *sine qua non* if we want

---

1. See also Whaling 1983: 167. This article by Whaling is in general very useful for giving an overview of different problems in comparative research.

to keep the perspective of the history of religions: It is the comparative perspective that lets us classify the phenomena and gives us our whole vocabulary; in short, it is that which constitutes our discipline.

Having stated the importance of comparison, I shall now turn to the question of how different kinds of comparative studies may contribute to the study of religion. For the moment it would be wise not to speak of "methods" because we are here concerned primarily with perspectives: Which religions are to be compared and for what purpose can we use the two types of comparisons that I shall discuss?

These two perspectives are the genetic and the typological. At this stage, they can only be defined loosely. In genetic comparisons, the object of investigation is a set of cultures related to each other by a cultural and/or historical connection. This connection may be common inheritance, which seems to be the case with the Indo-European cultures, or it could be based on close historical interrelationship, which is the case with Indian and Chinese religions. The connection may have ceased to exist a long time ago or it may be recent.

In typological comparisons, on the other hand, no such bonds exist between the cultures involved. To maintain that the dualism found in different schools of Gnosticism is very much the same as the dualism in Taoism involves a typological comparison (probably). And this goes much further; for instance, when a professor in comparative religion tells his students that sacrifice can be found all over the world, it is obvious that, although implicitly, he compares certain actions from different cultures and finds that they look alike and therefore can be labelled under the same designation.

I shall return to genetic comparisons below. First, however, let us consider some questions regarding typological comparisons: How do we explain the similarities found in different religions all over the world? And what do they imply for methodology?

Why do things look alike? Why is it that sacrifices all over the world are recognizable even though they vary very much in detail? These being human phenomena, we must rule out any explanation that invokes supernatural being(s).[2] Anyway, if this is the explanation, we do not know any scholarly approach that can reach it.

The way one explains similarities (and differences for that matter) is, however, a crucial point as regards method in the history of religions. If we go back more than a century, evolutionism dominated all the cultural sciences. The evolutionists noticed similarities and were able to give an answer to the "why", namely because all cultures at the same technological level would develop the same religious notions and customs, albeit with variation in detail. Both similarities and differences could thus be explained by referring to the level of evolution of the individual cultures. Similarities attested in cultures of different levels could be explained by the notion of "survival". It all seemed very plausible in the framework of evolutionism, and it had one very important consequence: One could interpret the "meaning" of a religious expression, whether ritual, mythic, artistic, or something else, based on similar phenomena attested in a comparable culture. By "meaning" in this connection, I refer to the overt associations, made by the worshippers in listening to the myth or in performing the ritual.[3] From the evolu-

---

2. To prevent misunderstandings, it must be emphasized that "supernatural beings" are an important component of any religious ideology, but ought not figure in scholarly accounts of objective reality.
3. This does obviously not imply that "meaning" can have no other connotations. It is a well known problem in the History of Religions that meaning is often used in mutually exclusive ways: Are we speaking of conscious or unconscious levels of the psyche? are we speaking of the interpretations made by religious specialists? are we speaking in functional terms (what does this symbol mean to the survival of the society in question, or what does it mean to religion as a whole) or in psychological terms etc?. It is definitely not my intention to sustain the widely held view not to say anything about meaning if the believers themselves cannot accept it. The actual point of my article, however, is how to deal with the relation between the symbolic expression and this more or less conscious level of understanding which we might, with Lawson and McCauley, call "implicit knowledge" (1990: 60 ff.) on the part of the believers. An interesting discussion on the subject "meaning", especially with reference to Wilhelm Dilthey, can be seen by Turner 1987: 95 ff.

tionist perspective, myths and rituals from ancient cultures, for which we have only scattered information, seemed to become perfectly clear when compared to similar information from better documented cultures.

Today we no longer believe that a more or less unilinear evolution took place in the psychic and cultural domain of man's existence. The matter seems to be much more complicated here than in biology, and the basic evolutionistic dogma that complex forms are always preceded by simpler ones is simply not the case. If we look at technologically inferior societies, we often see extremely complex systems of kinship, and there is no reason to believe that their religious outlook is any more simple.

Turning now to the more recent way of making typological comparisons, we shall look at the phenomenology of religion as represented by Mircea Eliade. Here, it is important to consider the notion of symbol, although we cannot discuss the question in detail.[4] However, what can be stated is that symbols have at least two aspects, namely an expression and a content. Even though they are not totally equivalent, we should also mention the semiotic terms "signifiant" and "signifié" as categories more or less akin to the expression/content-relation. It is obvious that the aspect of content is more complex than is often seen. It has normally several levels. If we take a simple example, we can mention the symbolism of death and resurrection in connection with initiation rituals as these have been analyzed by Eliade. Discussing one specific example, Eliade says (1975: 31):

> "Among the Makua the novices spend several months in a hut far from the village and are given new names; when they return to the village they have forgotten their family

---

4. An interesting discussion of the problems involved in symbolism can be read in Sperber 1975. Sperber's conclusion that symbols do not constitute codes and consequently have no meaning and can only be translated into other symbols seems rather convincing, although we are once again faced with the problem as to what is meant by "meaning".

> relationships. As Karl Weule puts it: by his stay in the bush, the son is dead in his mother's eyes. Forgetting is a symbol of death, but it can also be interpreted as betokening earliest infancy."

That 'forgetting' can signify the novice's death or his earliest infancy should be enough to warn us about being too hasty in our interpretations if we know only the overt expression. If death is the underlying referent of 'forgetting,' it can also become an expression for something else, a content in the second degree so to speak, namely of absolute finality. The relation here between expression and different levels of content is very complicated, as already mentioned, but the problem can be phrased as follows: Is there any stable relationship between expression and content? Whether the answer to this question is yes or no is of utmost importance for the comparative endeavor. If "yes", it allows us to maintain that when we find a symbolic expression and know its content, we can transfer this content to other cultures where we find similar expressions but have no access to the content. If "no", we do not have this possibility and in that case comparative investigations, and the phenomenology of religion in general, cannot tell us anything we do not already know concerning content.

Eliade himself was not very explicit about methodological matters. Apart from some vague statements about "archetypes", I have not been able to find any direct remarks concerning this problem.

Historians of religion have not had too much to say about this problem but it has played a major role in other disciplines. Especially in linguistics it is a common view nowadays that the relation between signifiant and signifié is arbitrary. Thus it is merely trivial to note that a "word" (the articulated expression, the sound picture) has one meaning in one language, whereas the same sound has quite a different meaning in another. If ritual, to take one example, may be seen as a kind of language, a ritual element, as for instance going out into the bush during initiation, can be taken similarly. Every individual culture may attach its own special meaning to this seclusion. The only common trait in initiatory seclusions is that they mark a difference from ordinary social life. Victor Turner's concept of liminality is very useful in this context (Turner 1969: 95 ff.) since it is an empty concept which gains its content only from being opposite to the nonliminal. The only universal semantic feature behind the ritual seclusion is simply that it is "different". I am not suggesting that the arbitrariness of the signifiant-signifié relation in language can be transferred directly to the ritual example, but the difference is only a matter of degree. It is reasonable to suggest, as has recently been done by Lawson and McCauley (1990: 62), that linguistic rules are more complicated than ritual rules simply because there are more elements to work with. In ritual (and myth, for that matter) there may be some iconic value in the expression but to judge this, it is necessary to know rather much of the semantic universe of the culture in question or of cultures strongly genetically related (a point to which I shall return). If this is not the case, it is not possible to draw any conclusions about the "meaning" of some ritual or mythological expression. There is thus no semantic essence universally applicable in relation to particular expressions. Let me illustrate this point by another example from Eliade. In his *Patterns in comparative Religion*, he deals with the symbolic form "tree" (1958: 265 ff.). In this connection he finds a number of connotations associated with this symbolic expression gathered from all over the world. These connotations are often more or less directly expressed in the religious texts themselves. However, we cannot assume the whole complex of connotations to be present whenever we come across a tree in a ritual or a myth. Again there are different levels of content. The most important connotation of the cross in Christianity is the death and resurrection of Christ, but this "meaning" is hardly present in any other religion, while the widespread connotation of "fertility" is pretty much absent from the Christian symbol, although it has been argued that the cross is only another version of an *axis mundi*.

What *can* be established is that the tree form is a good medium for thought and that it can be used to express concepts of fertility, stability, connecting links between heaven and earth, and many other concepts that people mythicize and deploy in ritual contexts. In some cultures the tree is polyvalent, whereas in others only a single or very few connotations are associated with this form. This means that semantic phenomenology, with Eliade as its most famous representative, can be seen only as a source of inspiration in order to investigate whether this or that connotation is present in a given context. Some of these connotations are "general" in the sense that they can be found in a number of religions all over the world, while others are fairly specific and may be confined to an individual culture or even to individuals within this particular culture (for instance poets and artists). "General" connotations are most likely to be explained by their iconic value (i.e. the vertical dimensions of the tree or any other "world-pillar" makes it suitable as a means of transport from earth to heaven, especially if the culture in question is of a "shamanic" type). Anyway, there is no reason to believe that the tree has any semantic essence from which all other meanings derive. Consequently the form "tree" can mean anything, and in order to decide its meaning, we must examine the semantic systems of the culture and religion in question. If we do not have this knowledge, no comparisons of a typological kind can help us to decide the meaning of any symbolic expression.

Wherever we meet a symbolic expression, we cannot assume an automatic link to some particular symbolic value. In other words: Typological comparisons cannot give us any answers regarding meaning and content, although they can be suggestive for posing relevant questions.

Turning to genetic comparisons, the situation is different. If we take as an example the comparative mythology of Georges Dumézil and his followers, it is obvious that here we are often dealing with parallels not only in expressions, but also in content. However, it is important to note the specific structural approach of Dumézil. He knows that the relation between a specific form and the specific content is arbitrary and that the "meanings" are not to be found at the level of elements but at that of structure, i.e. between relations. For example, only their position in the mythic structure permits him to identify the Nasatya in Indian mythology, the Vanir in Norse mythology and the Sabines in Roman legend as representative of the third function. There may be some common traits,[5] but they are relatively few, and the reason for positing similarity among these groups is their isomorphic relations to other entities in the cultural and mythological framework. The "meaning" and significance is thus to be sought in the relations among elements as part of the entire ideological framework.

Dumézil's results, establishing a common ideological framework among the historically known Indo-European peoples, are important in their own right, but also allow us to extrapolate from a better known to a lesser known, but genetically related culture area. This is the important difference between typological and genetic comparisons: As was said before we cannot accept that the content of similar expressions in two different cultures is necessarily similar. On the other hand, if the cultures involved have a common inheritance, the relation between content and expression, although still arbitrary in its basis, may be more or less stable.[6] This parallels the situation in linguistics, where it is common knowledge that often (but not always to be sure) common etymologically related words have the same content. Furthermore, we know of grammatical systems with different sound elements but with the systems as such being the same; the changes can be seen as transformations – as systematic

---

5. It is obvious that there are similarities between e.g. Thor and Indra and other gods of the second function at the level of both form and contents, but these are not decisive in the Dumézilian framework; warrior gods can be found all over the world, and they are naturally characterized by enormous strength and certain supernatural weapons. However, in the example just mentioned, there are other similarities in detail that can hardly be explained in any other way than by common inheritance. The best introduction to Dumézil's theory and results is *L'idéologie tripartie des Indo-Européens*.
6. As an example we could mention the war between the functions (Dumézil 1949: 115 ff.). From Dumézil's analysis it is obvious that this myth is dealing with the elements that is needed in order for a society to function.

changes and not arbitrary ones. It would be reasonable to assume the same relationship between the mythologies of the different Indo-European cultures, and Dumézil and his disciples have offered sufficient proof that this is the case.

The essential point is that in order to get an insight into the semantic content behind some symbolic form, through comparative investigations, there are two prerequisites. First, we must compare cultures related to each other historically, because it is likely that a stable relationship exists between morphology and content, as in comparative linguistics. Second, the material must be rich enough to allow us to see some structural features in at least one of the cultures involved in the comparisons; that means that there is a minimum limit as to the amount of information we need to have. If this is the case, we do have a methodological device based on theoretically acceptable claims to fill out lacunas in our material when making comparison, although this should still be done with great care.

In conclusion, I would argue that typological comparison is not a method at all, but a perspective from which it is possible to see similarities in morphology and, of course, in content where sufficient material is available. As such, it can help us to classify the different phenomena and can provide the scholarly study of religion with a metalanguage. However, it is not a method for interpretation, since typological similarities tell us nothing of the actual manifestations in individual religions. Typology helps the historian of religion in so far as no such thing as a science of religion could exist without classification or a general vocabulary and there would be no guidance for relevant questions. On the other hand, genetic comparison is certainly a perspective as well, but it is also a method that helps us understand the meaning and significance of symbolic expressions in a culture, even when sufficient material is not otherwise available.

All this may seem pretty trivial, but in many disciplines (archaeology and philology, e.g.) typological comparativism has often had a status as *the* key to all problems concerning meaning and content, which it certainly is not. On the other hand, it is my hope that I have argued sufficiently for the necessity of broad typological comparativism: Without comparing, there is no such discipline as the study of religion.

## Bibliography

Dumézil, Georges. 1949. *L'héritage Indo-Européen a Rome*. Paris.
–. 1958. *L'idéologie tripartie des Indo-Européens*. Bruxelles.
Eliade, Mircea. 1958. *Patterns in Comparative Religion*. New York.
–. 1975. *Rites and Symbols of Initiation. The Mysteries of Birth and Rebirth*. New York.
Lawson, E. Thomas and Robert N. McCauley. 1990. *Rethinking Religion. Connecting cognition and culture*. Cambridge, New York.
Sperber, Dan. 1975. *Rethinking Symbolism*. Cambridge.
Turner, Victor W. 1969. *The Ritual Process. Structure and anti-structure*. Ithaca.
–. 1987. *The Anthropology of Performance*. New York.
Whaling, Frank, ed. 1983. "Comparative Approaches." In *Contemporary Approaches to the Study of Religion*. Berlin, New York, Amsterdam.

# Levels of Comparison
# A Critical Approach to Thematization in Comparative Religion

*Jørgen Podemann Sørensen*
UNIVERSITY OF COPENHAGEN

All students of all kinds of Comparative Religion ought to perform their devotions over the following text by the sceptical philosopher Sextus Empiricus (c. A.D. 200), in which he compares the religious ideas and practices of quite a number of the peoples of antiquity:

> "… there is likewise great disagreement about sacrifices and the whole subject of the worship to be offered the gods. For what in some cults is considered holy in others is unholy, and this could never have been possible if the holy and the unholy were so by nature. For example, no one would think of sacrificing a pig to Sarapis, but they do sacrifice pigs to Heracles and Asclepius. It is unlawful to sacrifice a sheep to Isis, but to her who is called the Mother of the Gods, and to other gods as well, sheep are sacrificed with favourable omens. (…)
>
> The same sort of thing is to be seen in matters of human diet when viewed as religious observances. A Jew or an Egyptian priest would sooner die than eat pork. A Libyan deems it the gravest impiety to taste the flesh of a sheep. Some Syrians look thus upon the eating of doves …"[1]

---

1. Sextus Empiricus: *Outlines of Pyrrhonism,* III, 220 & 223, translated in Grant 1953

A lot of similar examples are given to demonstrate the impossibilty of generalizing in this field. It was the author's central idea that no universals exist and no generalization is possible, and in fact his whole work (4 volumes in the Loeb Classical Library) is devoted to refuting all kinds of generalization in all fields of human knowledge

As if nothing had happened, the first treatise on the phenomenology of religion, Sallustios' *On the Gods and the World*,[2] appeared only 150 years later. After a leap of some 1500 years, as if nothing had happened, similar treatises began to appear once more. The debate following this second *vogue* seems to indicate that there *are* problems in the comparative study of religions, which neither the *aisthêsis* of Sallustios nor the *epochê* of van der Leeuw could solve. Some of them had in fact been pointed out already by *Sextus Empiricus*. It is high time, then, that we face these problems and make a stand against the old sceptic. In so doing we shall, I hope, arrive at certain critical *prolegomena* to a future inventory of themes and categories in comparative religion.

The basic position of *Sextus*, that no universals exist, is shared by modern empirical science. And as far as symbolic universalism is concerned, I think that Sextus is rather succesful in demonstrating its impossibility. Focusing on any particular *motif*, comparison reveals only random differences, unless there is a genetic relationship between the examples we compare. In fact, to compare specific motifs is to investigate genetic bonds.

The comparison of motifs may, however, be contrasted with the comparison of *forms*. Forms are comparable only at a certain level of abstraction. At this level we compare sacrificial patterns, dietary rules, and food taboos, not pigs and sheep and doves. The borderline between motif and form is perhaps not always easy to draw, and constellations of motifs may also be regarded as formal patterns. Motif and form may be polarized, but they are not easily defined at the empirical level. The sole expedient

---

2. Sallustius 1961, translated also in Grant 1953

in this difficult situation is to define them at the level of inquiry, i.e. to distinguish types of comparison. To account for the distinction between motif and form – which we made in order to escape the antitheoretical spell of *Sextus Empiricus*, let us define two types of comparison:

> *Material comparison* aims at finding or proving genetic and historical relationships through the study of specific motifs and their distribution. Here belong studies of the number three in Indo-European religions as well as comparisons of the two-brother motif in ancient Egyptian and recent African myths and narratives.
>
> *Formal comparison* aims at developing analytic and descriptive notions and categories through the study of abstract structural similarities. This is where the phenomenology of religion belongs, even though some phenomenologists claim more lofty aims.

If we take into consideration also comparative studies of a more relational character, several more types may be distinguished. In this paper we shall deal only with the formal comparative study of religion. As a generalizing discipline, how does comparative religion – or the phenomenology of religion – respond to the skepticism of Sextus Empiricus? Or, to take advantage of the distinction between motif and form, has the discipline identified themes at a level of abstraction where comparison is posssible? There is no simple and straightforward answer to this question, but even a superficial glance at the inventories set up by the major treatises encompassing the whole discipline will reveal that no real and considerate stand has been made against the old skeptic. The most conspicuous case is Mircea Eliade's *Traité d'histoire des religions* or *Patterns in Comparative Religion,* as the English translation more modestly has it. By far the greater part of the *Traité* deals with symbolic patterns connected with nature: sky, sun, moon, water, stone, earth, woman, fecundity, vegetation. Within each chapter, there is a lot of fine analytic and comparative work concerning the logic that connects symbols, but the Pan-babylonian ancestry[3] of the whole underlying idea is clear enough: the great source of symbolism is the world of nature surrounding ancient man. There is a lot of subtle and abstract reasoning, but the thematizations that structure the greater part of the book are as concrete as the pigs of Sextus Empiricus – although, admittedly, broader and therefore permitting a certain amount of cross-cultural comparisons.

With a jump that passes unnoticed by its author, the tenth chapter of the *Traité* reaches a much higher level of abstraction: sacred space; and the remaining three chapters deal with matters of an even more abstract generality: sacred time, myth, and the structure of symbols. Perhaps we might say that the preceding excercises on celestial, solar, lunar, telluric, and other kinds of concrete symbolism were only there to prepare the insights of chapters 10 to 13; or we might, with G. Dumézil's preface to the French edition[4], infer that these fields of natural symbolism are not the real subject matter of the book; but the problem remains: at which level of abstraction is cross-cultural comparison possible and significant? Obviously, this problem did not exist for Mircea Eliade and other symbolic universalists; but I do think it is relevant to all non-universalist students of comparative religion.

In order to escape the challenge of Sextus Empiricus, we should not look for levels of comparison somewhere between heaven and earth; we should not, as it were, start at the pictorial end of symbolism, but go beyond telluric symbolism into subjects like sacred time, myth, etc. It is true that considerable cross-cultural similarities can be found in human attitudes to soil, fertility, and agriculture; it is also true that the physical and biological properties common to this whole field all over the earth may account for a certain cross-cultural uniformity of symbolism. But fertility symbolism is certainly not determined by

---

3. On the Pan-babylonian ancestry of some of Eliade's ideas, cf. Smith 1982, 26 ff and especially 1990, 15-16
4. Eliade 1970, 8 f.

agriculture alone; it is obviously conditioned by culture-specific symbolic systems: Earth as a deity was female in Greece, male in Egypt – for no conspicuous agricultural reason, but probably to fit into broader symbolic systems involving a comprehensive classification of male and female. Comparative thematizations departing from the pictorial end of symbolism are thus likely to reveal only random similarities and differences.

If not between heaven and earth, then perhaps *in* heaven? Eliade's chapter on celestial symbolism is populated by a truly cross-cultural assembly of celestial gods. Gods or 'conceptions of God' occupy a prominent position in comparative religion, and there is already a basis for Eliade's analysis in the learned world-wide studies of R. Pettazzoni[5]. The two eminent comparatists share an interest in the age of the conception of the high god without subscribing to any theory of 'Urmonotheismus'. Pettazzoni is quite programmatic on this point and emphasizes that his studies were "carried out on the two distinct but conjoined planes of phenomenology and of religious history, as complementary and inseparable factors of the science of religion in its essential unity."[6] I think we all agree that comparative and historical studies should somehow inform each other within our discipline, but Pettazzoni's *dictum* implies an idea of universal history, or even a history of specific types, which is not without difficulties. A type, since it is basically an abstraction, has no history; but it is, of course, a legitimate enterprise to examine and compare the different historical contexts in which conceptions of a certain type occur.

These considerations on the relationship between historical and comparative studies should also include the most 'historical' of all the treatises on the phenomenology of religion, Geo Widengren's *Religionsphänomenologie*.[7] Widengren makes no

---

5. Pettazoni 1956; 1922
6. Pettazzoni 1956, v, cf. 1954
7. Widengren 1969. The original, but somewhat shorter, Swedish edition: *Religionens värld*, appeared in 1945

claims towards universal history or symbolic universalism, but he has a chapter on "Der Gottesglaube: Das Wesen des Hochgottes", rich in examples from many parts of the world. In an article on methods in the phenomenology of religion,[8] he betrays that he considers such examples as "evidence", i.e. as somehow analogous to historical evidence. Since Widengren is strongly opposed to evolutionism, does not believe in universal history or Urmonotheismus, and is not concerned with proving the existence of God or gods, it is difficult to perceive the sense of "evidence" in this context. We might say at most that he considers examples indicative of the adequacy of a type or a theoretical concept – which is very much of a truism.

Seen in the perspective of the history of our discipline, these difficulties arise from the transposition of comparative methods from the "historical" constructions of panbabylonism and evolutionism into the new framework of the phenomenology of religion. Other difficulties, more immediately relevant to the present enquiry, seem to arise from thematization: To compare gods and attributes of gods is still somehow to thematize from the pictorial end of symbolism; and besides, it is to deal with beings to whom no single statue can do justice. Each single god has a name or at least a limited number of names, and sometimes there are iconographic conventions that help to identify him; but there is no critical way of penetrating the vast amount of myths, ritual texts, devotional tractates etc. to the true identity of a certain god. From a historical point of view, each invocation is in its own right and bears witness to the religion of its time and milieu. The matter is even more difficult: In his contribution in this volume, Tord Olsson demonstrates how the image of a god undergoes change according to the literary *genre* and speech situation in which it appears, even within the same time and milieu. What uncritical comparatists took as properties of a type of notion of god may be in fact properties of types of religious discourse. These types of discourse – myth, hymn, prayer etc. –

---

8. Widengren 1968

have a certain cross-cultural distribution, and their formal cross-cultural comparability was never seriously contested. But the uncritical comparatists went for the god and thus approached the data with a thematization made from the pictorial end of symbolism. This does not mean that comparative studies involving gods need be abolished; but it does mean that one cannot just pick and choose without distinguishing those types of discourse that shape the images of gods.

I hope now to have given an idea of the difficulties that motivate my endeavour to find or define levels of sufficient generality and abstraction to allow cross-cultural comparison. I believe the analogy of linguistics, the other comparative and cross-cultural discipline in the humanities, might help us to imagine the solution. Some early linguistic theories were concerned with the relation between sound and meaning, examining e.g. the hypothesis that the sound *i* is universally connected with smallness. There is really some comparative "evidence" to support this idea: little, piccolo, petit, minimus, mincemeat and what not. A few words like German 'Riese' and Greek 'gigas', both meaning 'giant' suffice to do away with universality in this case, and, needless to say, the idea that sound and meaning could be studied in this simple way has never found many adepts. In modern linguistics, admirable tools for analysis have been developed through the well known division into phonetics, morphology, syntax, and semantics. These disciplines represent levels of analysis, each one establishing its own set of rules. They are also levels of comparison: based on comparative studies, they also provide the framework within which significant comparative thematization may take place.

At a symposium on ritual in Åbo in 1991[9], I suggested that ritual be taken as such a distinct level of analysis, not to be confused with other levels. The alleged presence of evil spirits in the liminal period of a ritual is part of ritual economy and not evidence of a general fear of evil spirits. And what is said about

---

9. Sørensen 1993

the host in Christian churches is not belief, but ritual assignment. Leaps from the level of ritual to other levels or to religion in general may end up in obvious absurdities, give rise to new theories about exotic ways of thinking, or pass unnoticed. Along these lines I argued that ritual is a distinct level of analysis very much like the levels in linguistic theory. Since then, people have not ceased to ask me for other levels of analysis to be contrasted with or distinguished from that of ritual. And admittedly, this is exactly what is needed, if we are to proceed towards an orderly construction to replace the somewhat random inventory of the traditional treatises on the phenomenology of religion.

I have not, however, received any revelation of a complete, levelled construction of the object of comparative religion, and what I have to offer is nothing but considerations and suggestions. In attempting such a construction, incomplete and preliminary though it has to be, I would like to draw attention to a level which, unlike ritual, has no direct representation in religious expression. Behind all religious expressions within each single religion, there is a system of motifs, very much like the phonemic systems that can be worked out for each single language. Such phonemic systems account for the sounds and their possible combinations within a language. Speakers of the language are dependent on it, but not conscious of it as a system. The modern Egyptian transformation of Cleopatra and Ptolemaios into Kilopatra and Batalsa follows rules of such a system, but the average speaker is not able to account for these rules. In an analogous manner I imagine that behind every religion there is some such system of motifs and their possible combinations. Like the phonemic systems, it is a mere theoretical construct, which cannot be localized on the empirical level. Such a system of motifs is in fact no novel invention; it is what anthropologists call a system of classification. Classification is often said to be the way people arrange and divide their world, i.e. their cosmology; but the point I want to emphasize is that it should not be thought of as anything like a philosophical system. Cosmologies or classification systems exist only as *our* constructions of the cultural background from which the expressions we find at the empirical level may be derived.

The latent or merely theoretical level of cosmology is necessary, I believe, in order to define other levels which, like ritual, may be identified at the empirical basis. And here the analogy with linguistics ends, for the four levels I am going to suggest are to be regarded as articulations of cosmology for various purposes and accordingly with different formative principles. They are main types of religious discourse, and their mutual relationship is entirely different from the relationship between the linguistic levels, except for the important rule that shifts from one analytical level to another should never pass unnoticed.

**1. Ritual.** In the contribution I have already mentioned, I defined ritual as *representative acts designed to change or maintain their object*, thus focusing on efficacy as the formative principle of ritual. The point is that ritual is not information. Every bit of meaning and reference in ritual is there to effect the desired end – or we might say that in ritual, cosmology is put to work. Again, this is a strictly formal statement, which does not mean that ritual cannot serve social or psychological purposes. What it means is that ritual should not simply be taken as "the way people think", or "the way people act to each other".

**2. Mythical narrative.** Myth is traditionally viewed as a counterpart of ritual; and Levi-Strauss and Leach tend to consider myth and ritual as identical or as only two aspects of the same thing. There is probably some basic truth in this, but for analytical purposes, I find it useful to keep the two notions on two different levels. It is true that myth is often somehow represented in ritual, and ritual in myth, but there is a formal difference between narration and performance that matters in this respect. As ritual has it own rules, thus also narrative. And whereas the formative principle in ritual is efficacy, narrative is more straightforwardly a kind of communication; it addresses always a human receiver, who is informed by the narration. But like ritual, narrative is sequential; it exposes cosmology by arranging motifs in a pattern which is also a sequence that accounts for the continuities and the discontinuities of primeval and present, of present and eschatological time, of humans and gods. If narrative is thus a sequential articulation of cosmology as a logical pattern, it is as a sequence and a pattern that it should be studied. To pick out motifs, e.g. gods, and invest them with an autonomous personality around which evidence may be uncritically compiled, seems to me already a problematic affair in specific historical studies, and even more so in comparative studies.

**The Phantic Level.** In his chapter on myth, the first phenomenologist of religion, Sallustios, states that mind sees all things at once, but speech expresses some first and others after. This statement is not only meant to be very profound in a neoplatonic sense, it is in fact an intelligent observation on the sequential nature of myth, contrasted with something that is "all things at once." It might prove useful to distinguish a level that is not sequential as ritual and narrative, but akin to ritual in that it is not information, but pretends to be reality itself. I am not thinking of religious experience in the traditional broad psychological sense, but rather of religious performances and discourses claiming to represent a sudden breakthrough. This is where miracles, prodigies, revelation, and apocalypticism belong.

**The Deictic Level** is perhaps the one most easy to understand, but also one which has hardly been the object of comparative studies. It is the level of implementation of cosmology in preaching or religious argument, the level where cosmology is exposed as a strategy – for salvation, political action etc. etc.

The radical difference between the phantic and the deictic level may be illustrated by an amusing example: Some years ago I observed a graffito written with a silver speed-marker: JESUS IS ALIVE. Below this revelation had been added with a much less phantic pen: "Easter is cancelled." The graffito was not written in a railway station, but in the Theological Faculty of the University of Copenhagen, although in a humble place; and its pedestrian commentary does in fact admirably illustrate an important aspect of religious polemics. Quite a lot of the enormous amount of religious polemics that has come down to us from different religions and historical periods involves the inability or the refusal to consider a religious expression on its proper level. In his important book *Demystifying Mentalities,* G.E.R. Lloyd[10] demonstrates that the ancient Greek distinction between *mythos* and *logos* is, in its origin as a distinction, a polemical one. Those who understand themselves as *logikoi* in late Classical and Hellenistic Greece, e.g. Hippocratics opposed to traditional magico-religious healers, are in fact people who expose classification systems – like the four bodily fluids – as a strategy. And they are the ones who use *mythos* and *mageia* as polemical terms in a struggle that has often pathetically been thought of as the origin of modern science – but which is in fact nothing but a confrontation of discourses on the deictic level with those on the mythic and ritual level.

I am aware that by roughly delineating these four levels of analysis I have not done much more than confess my belief that a construction of levels as modes of articulation of cosmology is possible and desirable in the formal comparative study of religions. There is still much to do before we arrive at a well argued construction, and ultimately, a revelation might be necessary. The point that I want to make is that without such a levelled construction as a framework for comparative thematizations, the risk of uncritical compilation around some favourite idea is considerably greater. To be critical in this respect is precisely to distinguish such levels.

---

10. Lloyd 1990, 44 ff.

# Bibliography

Eliade, Mircea. 1970. *Traité d'histoire des religions.* Paris.
Grant, Frederick C. 1953. *Hellenistic Religions.* New York.
Lloyd, G.E.R. 1990. *Demystifying Mentalities.* Cambridge.
Pettazzoni, Raffaele. 1922. *Dio* I, Roma.
–. 1956.*The All-knowing God.* London.
–. 1954. "Apperçu introductif", *Numen* 1, pp. 1-7.
Sallustios. 1961. *Des dieux et du monde.* ed. G. Rochefort. Paris.
Smith, Jonathan Z. 1982 *Imagining Religion.* Chicago.
–. 1990. *To Take Place.* Chicago.
Sørensen, J. Podemann. 1993. "Ritualistics: a New Discipline in the History of Religions", in *The Problem of Ritual.* ed. by Tore Ahlbäck. Åbo.
Widengren, Geo. 1968. "Some remarks on the Methods of the Phenomenology of Religion", *Acta Universitatis Upsaliensis* 17, 1968, pp. 250-260.
–. 1969. *Religionsphänomenologie.* Berlin. The original, but somewhat shorter, Swedish edition: *Religionens värld,* appeared in 1945.

# Speaking of Purity:
# When the Zoroastrian High Priest first met the Hindu Rajah

*Alan V. Williams*
DEPARTMENT OF RELIGIONS AND THEOLOGY
UNIVERSITY OF MANCHESTER, UK

## Introduction

The modern Westerner tends to think of matters of bodily conduct and hygiene as personal and private, and might therefore assume that in religion, too, matters of purity and pollution are, and always have been, better kept to oneself and out of sight. The student of the history of religions knows well, however, that this is not so, especially since Mary Douglas turned on the searchlight of anthropological scrutiny of the subject in her *Purity and Danger* in 1966. In this paper I present an example from a popular, old, Zoroastrian text, where matters which are considered distinctly taboo in modern western culture, namely the states of menstruation, parturition and miscarriage/stillbirth, are brought forward in a quite unselfconscious, indeed one could say, almost ostentatious way. The passage I discuss is part of an exchange between a Zoroastrian *dastur* ('high priest') and a Hindu rajah in the Persian Zoroastrian verse text the *Qissa-ye Sanjān*. After a brief analysis of the passage some reasons for the inclusion of these matters in their first encounter are considered.

## Purity as a Problem

Like other modern people, Zoroastrians, especially the Parsis of India and the diaspora in western cities of the world, have a public and personal problem with the notion of what is pure and what is polluting. They are divided among themselves into roughly two opposing groups. On the one hand there are those who regard themselves as 'traditionalists', who see themselves as 'orthodox': they attempt to adhere as scrupulously as possible to the daily ritual observances and lifelong practices which are recorded in Zoroastrian oral tradition, both lay and priestly, and which are backed up by a body of priestly texts, written in the ancient Iranian languages, Avestan and Pahlavi, and medieval Zoroastrian Persian. On the other hand there is a large grouping of Zoroastrians who assert the need to reinterpret their religious traditions, to make them applicable to a modern world which has changed greatly from the past in India or in Iran; even to break with certain practices which they regard as primitive, benighted and belonging only to the past. With their progressive, reformist reinterpretations of Zoroastrian religion they are seen to be pulling further and further away from the first group, the traditionalists. Some of these latter, for example priests in high positions in India, have expressed the sentiment that it would be better for the religion to be split into two distinct parts than for the reformists to win the day. Much of the heated polemic which has been hurled between these two camps in the course of this century has been over issues such as intermarriage and attempts at conversion by non-Zoroastrians into the religion. The disputes have been about how to set the boundaries of where the religion begins and ends, what and whom it includes, and how much jurisdiction the religion should have over the lives of women and men, boys and girls.

The 'debates' (if such a sober term can be used for the vicious exchanges of intra-community disputes) have often been connected with, and even expressed in terms of, conflicting presentations of doctrine and practice concerned with purity and pollution, and the doctrine of evil (*i.e.* the question of whether or not Zoroastrianism is a religion of metaphysical dualism, ethical dualism, or is not dualistic at all). Purity, pollution and the doctrine of evil have an elaborate mythological symbolism in Zoroastrianism and are three themes-in-one which form an index of many conflicts and tensions in the community world-wide. Each camp uses textual reference, theological argumentation and a whole panoply taken from learned religious tradition of the past. To an outsider it is curious to see how much disputation the language of purity and pollution can express, even within an apparently secularized, urbanized community, in Los Angeles, London or Bombay.

## Purity codification as a basis of Zoroastrianism

In traditional Zoroastrianism (*i.e.* that which we find in texts and traditions from the pre-modern era before the early part of the 19th century) purity has an elaborate codification which defines, ranks and categorizes everything within and without the community of *behdins* 'those of the Good Religion', from the gods and demons and their cosmic history down to human beings and the minutiae of earthly life. Thinking about purity defines order against chaos, lays down the lines of the community, and determines who is a Zoroastrian, and who is not. For much of their history Zoroastrians have resorted to strict purity rules to regulate and perpetuate their own community survival in a hostile environment (*viz.* Muslim Iran from the 7th cent. CE) or in a complex and competitive, supposedly 'neutral', environment (Hindu-Muslim India since the 8th cent. CE). Purity has an enormous symbolic burden to bear, which has been given even greater religious (as opposed to social or community) significance because of the strongly dualistic cast of Zoroastrian theology in its classical formulation in the Pahlavi books. Whereas in Brahminism there is an explicitly social dimension to the acting out of purity rules according to one's *jāti* and *varna*, and whereas in Judaism, Islam and Christianity many other religious themes function to strengthen the boundaries of community (incontrovertible written scripture, jurisprudence, credal formulae, etc.), for Zoroastrianism purity is central and perhaps paramount. Without purity there is no religion, because there can be no *yasna*, 'worship' of God, and without purity one is little better than the evil one is taught to smite. Purity is coterminous with the good and the holy.[1] Purity expresses exactly one of the fundamental ideas of Zoroastrian cosmology, that prior to mortal existence, which is a mixture of good and evil, there was a spiritual unmixed state of existence. That which is spiritual is unmixed, whether it be good or evil, with its opposite (though, significantly 'pure' is exclusively an attribute of the good, never evil). To be real and embodied in this physical world is to exist in a 'mixed' state. Zoroastrian doctrine teaches the human mission to *un*mix this world by invoking and embodying the power of the good, unmixed spiritual world of the gods (Pahlavi *amahraspand*s, *yazad*s) and their helpers (*hamkār*s). A theological imperative is translated into actual practice in ritual observance and a code of behaviour and ethics, in a tradition which looks back to the visionary reforms of its ancient prophet, 'righteous Zoroaster' (Avestan Ašo Zarathuštra).

In spite of the importance given to the code of purity in Zoroastrianism, relatively few academic students have paid attention to its structure and significance in the tradition. Indeed Iranian studies in general (as with some other developing fields which do not have Biblical but rather strategic[2] affiliations) has been preoccupied with the preliminary work of learning the ancient and modern languages, with establishing the texts, putting them into a historical context, and with other tasks on the agenda of what Robert Alter has called 'excavative' activity.[3] Scholars have laboured for many years at the Herculean task of editing and translating the Zoroastrian texts and complementary evidence of rock inscriptions, yet with a few notable excep-

---

1. E.g. Pahlavi *pāk* 'pure' may also be rendered 'holy'; in Zoroastrian Persian *pāk* is frequently the synonym of Arabo-Persian words for 'holy'; in Muslim Persian it comes to mean predominantly, if not exclusively 'holy', *viz.* Pākistān 'Holy Land'.
2. *i.e.*, 'orientalist' in the sense made notorious by Edward Said.
3. 1981:13 '"excavative" – either literally, with the archaeologist's spade and reference to its findings, or with a variety of analytic tools intended to uncover the original meaning of biblical words, the life situations in which specific texts were used, the sundry sources from which longer texts were assembled.'

tions, this has been driven more by the quest for philological and archaeological knowledge rather than by that of the historian of religions. At a certain stage of the interpretation of religious texts, as in the study of the Bible, it is realized that we ignore at our peril the work of literary scholars and social scientists.

However little impact her work may have made on other Iranologists, Mary Douglas's work on purity and pollution made new sense to me of the strict and clearly stated oppositions of Zoroastrian cosmology, theology and ritual practice. In an article published in 1989 I observed that previous attempts to discuss the Zoroastrian schema of purity and pollution rules had been based either on medical materialism, explaining everything in terms of hygiene, or on theological/ethical grounds which equate the pure and the polluted simply with the morally good and the morally evil. At first the texts and rites concerning purity which they describe may seem dull fare for modern tastes. However, when they are examined systematically the rules of purity of Zoroastrianism are analogous to a complex 'board-game' of cosmology and eschatology. In spite of obvious parallels with apparently similar purity systems of Brahminism and Judaism, there are deep and important differences, I suggested, because of the thoroughgoing dualism of Zoroastrian thought in the Pahlavi texts. Binary coding is in operation at every level of thought and so these purity and pollution rules are closer to an ideal type of Douglas's explanation of the body as symbolic of social boundary protection.[4] It is not sociological reductionism to say that the body is a symbol of Zoroastrian society. Douglas's dictum that 'the powers and dangers credited to the social structure (are) reproduced in small on the human body'[5], is, once translated out of sociological terminology, a clear principle of the code of rules about purity and pollution in traditional Zoroastrian texts.

---

4. See for example Douglas 1966:115.
5. Ibid. *loc.cit.*

ALAN V. WILLIAMS

## The *Qissa-ye Sanjān*

That we should find rules and pronouncements about ritual purity and about pollution of the sacred elements is perhaps to be expected in 'priestly' texts such as the 9th cent. CE Pahlavi books. It is more surprising to find such matters at the centre of a popular text. The text in question, the *Qissa-ye Sanjān*, is beloved by the Zoroastrian community to this day. It tells of their journey from Iran to Gujarat in India long ago (for this is a story not a history), and their settlement and success in the subcontinent. Yet, few Parsis know the actual text, either in English, Gujarati or the original Persian, since the outlines of the story are so well known in oral tradition in the community. In editing the text for publication I have had some difficulty in locating manuscripts and even printed versions of the text.

The *Qissa-ye Sanjān* is a narrative of some 430 couplets, in reasonably good Persian poetry, said to have been composed by a *dastur* called Bahman about 1600 CE. Yet Bahman himself acknowledges that the story is a traditional one:

> *Now listen to the wonderful tales from the lore of the mobads and ancient sages*[6]

Bahman says he himself heard the story from another *dastur*:

> *One day he told us this story, beautifully he strung together the pearls of past events*[7]

The author relates how, as the prophet Zarathuštra predicted, the religion would thrive a long time under the protection of glorious rulers and holy priests, but eventually at the end of the dynasty of Sasanian kings, would be brought low by the coming of the Muslims[8]:

---

6. 1.64.
7. 1.74.
8. The Persian word used for Muslims in Zoroastrian texts is *juddin*, a generic

*When the kingship left King Yazdegar, when the juddins came and took his throne,*
*Iran was shattered from that time. Alas for that kingdom of the Faith which had fallen to ruin!*
*At that time all those who kept their hearts true to the Zand and Pāzand were dispersed,*
*When every single one of the behdins and dasturs suddenly went into hiding for the sake of the Religion;*
*They abandoned their abodes, their lands, gardens, villas and palaces all for the sake of their Religion.*

As the story goes, the Zoroastrians fled to a mountainous region of Iran for a hundred years, then to the city of Hormuz on the southern coast of Iran. Eventually, having consulted the astrological tables, a wise priest declares:

*'...Our subsistence has come to an end*
*It is right if we leave this land. Now we must go forth from this kingdom,*
*Or else we shall all fall into a trap, wisdom will be useless, it will be an unwise decision.*
*So it is better that we must go from the wicked demons toward Hind.*
*In fear of our lives and for the sake of the religion let us all flee to Hind henceforth.'*

They set sail and arrived on an island off the coast of India, where they stayed for nineteen years. Only then did they make the short crossing to mainland India, during which they were caught up in a violent storm at sea. They were delivered from danger by the intervention of God (Persian *xudā*) who heard their prayers and their promise to establish a sacred fire dedicated to the tutelary god Bahrām (Avestan Verethraghna). They reach the town of Sanjān and, as the text says:

---

term whose literal meaning 'those of other religion' appears neutral, but in fact is as derogatory as English 'heathen', or Arabic *kāfir*.

> *In that place there was a good rajah, whose mind was opened to holiness.*
> *His name was Jādi Rāna; he was generous, intelligent and learned.*
> *The dastur went before him with gifts: he (i.e. the dastur) was renowned for his knowledge and wisdom.*
> *He paid his respects to him and said: 'O rajah of rajahs, grant us a place in this city.*
> *We are strangers having come to you for refuge in your city and place.*
> *We have come to this place for the sake of religion: we have heard that there is a rajah*
> *He is descended from the Shāh Rāyān, of virtuous deeds, who is famed throughout Hind*
> *Who will give refuge in his city and kingdom, who looks upon their condition with compassion.*
> *We became happy at this news: we have come before you with good omens.*
> *Now we have come to your land, putting our hope in you we have escaped the wicked ones'.*[9]

The rajah, however, is taken aback by the new arrivals:

> *Fear for his throne entered his heart thinking 'they will sack this country'.*
> *He was frightened by their robes and vestments: secretly he wanted to ask the dastur about hidden things.*
> *Then he said: 'O devout dastur, first tell us the secrets of these matters.*
> *Then (tell us) what are the customs of your religion, what is hidden and what is manifest.*
> *First I shall look at your religion: later we shall grant you your place.*[10]

---

9. ll. 137-146.
10. ll. 149-153.

Before the *dastur* is allowed to answer, the rajah lays down four other conditions, which stipulate (1) that they should give up speaking Persian for 'the language of the kingdom of Hind', (2) that their women should dress as Indian women do, (3) that they should not bear arms, and (4) that they should marry in a certain way. At this point the text depicts the *dastur* as making a speech which outlines the Zoroastrian identity and religion. It is a most revealing passage, as much for what it excludes as for what it includes. First the *dastur* reassures the rajah that they are a peace-loving people:

> *The old mobad then spoke to him: 'I speak of the religion, listen, o sagacious rājah.*
> *Do not be distressed on account of us: ill shall never come from us in this place.*
> *We are friends of all of Hindustan: we shall everywhere scatter the heads of your adversaries'.*[11]

He then explains why they have left their homeland:

> *'Know for certain that we worship God: for the sake of the Religion we fled the wicked ones.*
> *We have forsaken all we had: many hardships befell us on the way.*
> *We have left all our homes and our property and possessions, o fortunate king'.*[12]

At this point he must answer the rajah's first question and reveal 'the customs of your religion':

> *We strangers are of the line of Jamshid: we respect the moon and the sun.*
> *Three others we hold dear: the cow, and water and fire for the sake of its light.*
> *We revere fire and water, likewise the cow, the sun and moon.*

---

11. ll. 161-163.
12. ll. 164-166.

170  *God has created everything in the world and we revere it because he has chosen it.*
*Likewise we tie on our kusti of 72 threads, and we recite holy words by heart.*
*Our women who have their period do not look at the sun or sky or moon.*
*They keep far away from water and fire because they have the quality of light.*
*They strictly avoid everything, in the bright day and dark night.*
175  *She sits thus until the menstruation has left her: when she washes her head she may (again) look at fire and the sun.*
*Again that woman who gives birth to a child must sit apart for 40 days.*
*The exclusion resembles that of menstruation. She abstains: that is not contemptible*
*When the child is born of a woman in a few months or that child is stillborn,*
*She may go nor hurry anywhere: she may converse with nobody.*
180  *That woman also must practise great abstinence: she must sit for 41 days in this state.'*[13]

The speech ends here in the text, which adds:

*He described to him one by one all the other customs and practices. When the hidden things of the religion were spoken in elegant manner, the pearls of discourse were strung.*
*When the Hindu rājah heard the good speech of the dastur ... his heart became completely composed.*[14]

## Analysis of the passage

The actual report of what was said to the rajah occupies only 14 couplets (167-180) of the text. At first sight it is puzzling why the *dastur* should mention these particular matters, from among

---

13. ll. 167-180.
14. ll. 181-183.

the great array of distinguishing features of Zoroastrian religion, to a Hindu (*i.e. juddin*) rajah (*i.e.* male, royal). No mention is made of the prophet Zarathushtra, the name of God Ahura Mazda, nor his Beneficent Immortals (Ameša Spentas) nor the other major doctrines concerning heaven, hell, the judgment and afterlife, nor indeed the many things that are done in the religion in this life. However, it can be shown that the passage breaks down into two sets of three statements (§), which I number as follows:

§1 ll. 167-8: their lineage and their five objects of reverence in the order: moon, sun, cow, water, fire;
l. 169: objects of reverence again, in exact reverse order: fire, water, cow, sun, moon;
§2 l. 170: a theological statement about God the creator and the reason for man's reverence of the created world;
§3 l. 171: mentions the rite of 'tying the kusti';
§4 ll. 172-175: women in menstruation must not look at or touch the sacred elements;
§5 ll. 176-177: women after parturition must sit apart and abstain (*i.e.* from the world)
§6 ll. 178-180: women after failed parturition (miscarriage or stillbirth) may go nowhere and speak to no one.

It had first struck me as peculiar that of these 14 couplets of description of the religion, 9 should be about apparently gynaecological matters. This, however is to read the text anachronistically and without understanding what is being encoded into the language of purity rules concerning women. §§1-3 are concerned with religion in terms of reverence, the origin and order of things, and ritual practice (*kusti* and prayers). Women do not feature in this part of the speech. §§4-6 are statements concerned with women exclusively. There is a strong parallelism and connection, however, to the first group of statements.

§4 refers back to §1, mentioning how women must avert their gaze from sun and moon, and keep themselves far away from water and fire. In other words, the sources of purity and light in §1 are contrasted with what is stated as *the* source of pollution of those elements in §4.

Similarly, in §2 God is affirmed to be the creator of everything in the world, which is therefore deserving of reverence, whereas in §5 women who have given birth to a new life must abstain from looking and touching the sacred elements mentioned in §1, just like the polluting menstruating woman in §4.

Lastly, in §6 the woman who has miscarried must be completely constrained, in her movement and in her speech. This corresponds to the mentioning of symbolic tying of the kusti girdle and reciting of holy words in §3. Zoroastrian women in the three conditions mentioned in this passage are in fact traditionally called *bi namāz* 'without prayer' because they are forbidden to utter holy words for a specified duration.

# Conclusion

The speech is said to have had the desired effect of reassuring the rajah and the intended result of finding the Zoroastrians a new home. The *dastur*'s words in the first three §§ reassured the rajah not only that their religion was not so very dissimilar to his own, *viz.* reverence for these elements, recognition of a creator god, and mention of the sacred thread so visible in Brahminism. The latter three §§ emphasise that this religion is practised and made efficacious in Zoroastrian society, *i.e.* not just in the temple precincts. By stating that their womenfolk are well controlled by the religion, the *dastur* tacitly communicates that their religion is one which does not shrink from imposing a rigorous order of purity, hierarchy, and law in general, upon the community it governs. The passage emphasises to the rajah that, as Zoroastrians are wont to say, they are well behaved not only in thought and word, but in deed also.

The remaining question of why the *dastur* chose to speak about the purity of *women* and did not mention the many controls upon the purity of men which are encountered in Zoroastrian texts, is probably best answered, in a paper of this length, by my risking a hypothesis which must remain undiscussed until another day: in Zoroastrian texts stipulations about the maintenance of purity with regard to male bodily functions, and especially their sexual activity, were rules which were read as being particular to men and perhaps closer to the modern sense of 'private and personal'. In contrast, however, stipulations about the purity of women were understood to be a shorthand way of referring to the problems of regulating organic, and specifically sexual, life in general. Such was the symbolic burden carried by the woman: her 'purity' was very much a public matter of concern, as we have seen.

## Bibliography

Alter, R, 1981 *The Art of Biblical Narrative*, Basic Books Inc., New York
Boyce, M 1975 *A History of Zoroastrianism*, vol. 1, Brill, Leiden
Douglas, M. 1966 *Purity and Danger: an analysis of concepts of pollution and taboo*, Routledge and Kegan Paul, London
–. 1975 *Implicit Meanings: Essays in Anthropology*, Routledge and Kegan Paul, London
Neusner, J. 1973 *The Idea of Purity in Ancient Judaism*, Brill, Leiden
–. 1994 *Purity in Rabbinic Judaism: a systemic account*, South Florida Studies in the history of Judaism, Atlanta Georgia
Williams, A.V. 1989 'The Body and the Boundaries of Zoroastrian Spirituality', *Religion* 19: 227-239
–. 1990 *The Pahlavi Rivāyat Accompanying the Dādestān ī Dēnīg*, Det Kongelige Danske Videnskabernes Selskab, Historisk-filosofiske Meddelelser 60:1&2, Munksgaard, Copenhagen
–. 1994 'Zoroastrian and Judaic Purity Laws: Reflections on the viability of a sociological interpretation' in Shaked S. and Netzer, A (eds.) *Irano-Judaica III*, Ben-Zvi Institute, Jerusalem
–. 1997 'Zoroastrianism and the Body' in Coakley, S. (ed.) *Religion and the Body*, Cambridge Studies in Religious Traditions 8, Cambridge University Press, Cambridge
–. forthcoming 1999 *The Zoroastrian Qissa-ye Sanjān*